# STAY SAFE

### Be Aware and Prepared at Home, at Work, and on the Street

Ronald A. Rufo, EdD

*To Victoria,*
*A beautiful person with a wonderful heart. I hope you enjoy my book.*
*Stay safe,*
*Ron*

# Advance Praise for
## *Stay Safe: Be Aware and Prepared at Home, at Work, and on the Street*

"I feel everyone should read Dr. Ron Rufo's book *Stay Safe: Be Aware and Prepared at Home, at Work, and on the Street.* He has provided an incredible amount of amazing advice and brilliant tips in his book to keep communities across our country safe. Knowledge is everything. Ron takes his former police experience and knowledge as a crime prevention speaker to a new level. His goal is to prevent crime and educate everyone on how not to become a victim. Ron's book elaborates on how a person can protect themselves and their neighbors. He gives us tips we may never have thought about. Life is an ongoing educational process, and to have a book like Ron's that explains the value of trusting gut feeling and common sense is immeasurable. I highly recommend Dr. Ron Rufo's book—it is a must-read for everyone."
   *Andrew J. Hock, deputy chief of police, Elmwood Park, Illinois*

"Life is about educating yourself. Dr. Ron Rufo is not only a friend of mine but has done an outstanding job in *Stay Safe* to educate everyone on how to stay safe. He explains the do's and don'ts about public safety and the littlest things that people do not think of. Ron gives us many fine examples of how we must pay attention to our surroundings. His book highlights many issues that I hear about at community meetings in my ward. I want to thank Dr. Ron Rufo for providing us with the necessary tools that we need today."
   *Nick Sposato, alderman for the 38th Ward in the City of Chicago*

"In Dr. Ron Rufo's book *Stay Safe: Be Aware and Prepared at Home, at Work, and on the Street*, he has laid out a clear path to staying safe in today's unsafe world. Throughout my career, I have taught individuals that to avoid being a victim, they must "have a plan" before they need it. Ron has laid out a common-sense set of guidelines to get the reader thinking about their safety before they become a victim. *Stay Safe* is a must-read for you, your family, friends, employees, and anyone you care about."

***Fernando "Frank" Flores, commander (retired) Illinois State Police***

"Dr. Ron Rufo has done an excellent job writing this book about the many components of safety that many people take for granted. The purpose for writing this book was to create the awareness that people must make themselves less vulnerable and less likely to be victimized. Ron emphasizes that citizens must be prepared and informed to secure themselves and their property with limited involvement of law enforcement. Dr. Rufo accentuates that simple things like understanding how to increase personal safety or identifying weaknesses and limitations in existing security measures are a start on that journey."

***Captain John Doherty of the Chicago Police Department***

"Dr. Ron Rufo gives sound, practical guidance to help you stay safe on the streets today. His decades of police experience on the mean streets of Chicago, combined with his academic credentials, make him uniquely qualified to provide useful tips to better enable the reader to stay safe every day. A significant increase in street crime is being seen across the nation, and the information provided by Dr. Rufo can play a crucial role in helping to keep you and your loved ones safe."

***Patrick Murphy, chief of police,
Springfield Park District Police Department***

"Recent increases in crime are on everyone's mind. Dr. Ron Rufo uses his extensive police background to provide clear and usable suggestions to help reduce the likelihood that we are victimized. Ron is a renowned crime prevention expert who has spent his career helping keep our community safe by giving over 300 safety presentations a year. *Stay Safe, Be Aware and Prepared at Home, at Work, and on the Street* includes the best of his recommendations for personal safety that will help the reader improve their mindset and take responsibility for their own safety. He outlines simple, clear guidelines for all of us to follow. Ron leaves no stone unturned, and I highly recommend his book to anyone who wants to improve their safety."

*Dave Anderson, chief of police, City of Des Plaines, Illinois*

"Dr. Ron Rufo's book *Stay Safe, Be Aware and Prepared at Home, at Work, and on the Street* is an excellent source of information for everyone. He provides different scenarios that enlighten the reader by giving insight into how to prevent being a victim. Ron is not only a great speaker but has written several books that help police officers with everyday issues. I have seen Ron speak and read his books, and all I can say is you will *not* be disappointed at all reading his latest book or if you get to see him speak. Ron, thank you for your hard work and dedication to helping everyone stay safe."

*Sgt. Daniel Banicki, St. Joseph County Police Department, South Bend, Indiana*

"While violent crimes tend to get the lion's share of media attention and instill fear and trepidation, the panoply of other crimes, while not as newsworthy, impact their victims just as significantly. In *Stay Safe*, Dr. Ron Rufo hits the nail on the head, addressing everything from timeless scams such as fortune-telling and phony bank examiners to surviving an active shooter. His treatment of the emerging crime trends in the cyberspace and worlds of cryptocurrency will serve to not only alarm but also educate readers about things that heretofore only previous victims or police officers were aware of. Now, more than ever, education and information about active shooters, scams, and other crimes is crucial."

*Bill Kushner, retired chief of police, DesPlaines, Illinois*

"*Stay Safe* reflects Dr. Ron Rufo's commitment and dedication to keeping everyone safe. Ron outlines in detail what should and shouldn't be done in many confrontational situations. *Stay Safe* is a very informative book that everyone should own."

*Retired Chicago Police Sergeant Tim Capparelli*

"Dr. Ron Rufo is a true public servant who pours his heart and passion into his work and educating others. If you're looking to expand your perspective and listen to an experienced professional, this book is for you."
***Brandon Griffith, Founder & CEO, Griffith Blue Heart Nonprofit, Deputy Sheriff Pinal County Sheriff's Office***

"Ron's message to 'Always trust your instincts!' is so important right now. Even people who generally have a decent awareness of their surroundings will gain insights into how a criminal seeks out their prey. With these important messages and examples, Ron continues to serve and protect the public, even though he retired from the force many years ago."
***Roger Bay, retired commander 16th District, Chicago Police Department***

"Throughout his distinguished career, Dr. Rufo was known as an officer who was able to weave his street experience together with the best thinking available to educate the community he served on effective strategies to prevent them from becoming the victim of a crime. He realized that to be effective, advice has to be applied in the environment of the issue. In *Stay Safe*, Dr. Rufo addresses the points that people need to consider and the things they need to do for their families and themselves to minimize the risk of becoming a victim in these unsettled times. His thoughtful strategies and sound advice, based on his decades of experience, deserve your full attention."
***Eugene Roy, retired chief of detectives, Chicago Police Department***

# STAY SAFE

## Be Aware and Prepared at Home, at Work, and on the Street

Ronald A. Rufo, EdD

Stay Safe: Be Aware and Prepared at Home, at Work, and on the Street

© 2023 Ronald Rufo, EdD

All Rights Reserved

No part of this publication may be reproduced, stored in a retrieval system, or transmitted in any form or by any means, electronic, mechanical, photocopying, recording, scanning, or otherwise, without the prior written permission of the author.

Limit of Liability/Disclaimer of Warranty: This publication is designed to provide accurate and authoritative information in regard to the subject matter covered. It is sold with the understanding that neither the author nor the publisher is engaged in rendering legal, investment, accounting, medical, or other professional services. While the publisher and author have used their best efforts in preparing this book, they make no representations or warranties with respect to the accuracy or completeness of the contents of this book and specifically disclaim any implied warranties of merchantability or fitness for a particular purpose. No warranty may be created or extended by sales representatives or written sales materials. The advice and strategies contained herein may not be suitable for your situation. You should consult with a professional when appropriate. Neither the publisher nor the author shall be liable for any loss of profit or any other commercial damages, including but not limited to special, incidental, consequential, personal, or other damages.

AMR Publishers

ISBN 13: 978-1-7362021-1-1

Credits:
Cover design by Ronald Cruz
Editing by Candace Johnson, Change It Up Editing
Interior design by Jera Publishing

Chapter opening quotations
BrainyQuote.com
QuoteFancy.com

Chapter opening quotes are from the following sites:
Chapter 1 Quotes.com
Chapters 2, 11 Goodreads.com
Chapters 3, 4 Brainyquote.com
Chapter 6 Twitter.com/tinybuddha
Chapters 7, 8 Quotefancy.com
Chapter 9 Quotetab.com
Chapter 10 SafetyCulture.com
Chapter 11 AZquotes.com

I dedicate this book to my beautiful and wonderful granddaughter, Alinah. She is kind, thoughtful, and considerate. I am proud to be her "Papa."

To my daughters Rita, Laura, and Cara, who bring joy to my heart; I love them each in my own special way. They have brought many years of joy and happiness into my life, and I am so proud to be their dad.

To my wife, Debbie, who has brought happiness into my life from the first day that we met. She inspires me to always do my best and reach for the stars and never look back. I am blessed.

*"Safety applies with equal force to the individual, to the family, to the employer, to the state, the nation and to international affairs. Safety, in its widest sense, concerns the happiness, contentment and freedom of mankind."*

William M. Jeffers, former president,
Union Pacific Railroad Co.

## Contents

Foreword . . . . . . . . . . . . . . . . . . . . . . . . . . . . . . . . . . . . . . . . . . . . . xv
Introduction . . . . . . . . . . . . . . . . . . . . . . . . . . . . . . . . . . . . . . . . . . . 1
1  Street Safety . . . . . . . . . . . . . . . . . . . . . . . . . . . . . . . . . . . . . . . 5
2  How to Describe a Person . . . . . . . . . . . . . . . . . . . . . . . . . . . 42
3  ATMs . . . . . . . . . . . . . . . . . . . . . . . . . . . . . . . . . . . . . . . . . . 48
4  Pickpockets . . . . . . . . . . . . . . . . . . . . . . . . . . . . . . . . . . . . . . 52
5  Identity Theft and Credit Card Fraud . . . . . . . . . . . . . . . . . . 56
6  Scams . . . . . . . . . . . . . . . . . . . . . . . . . . . . . . . . . . . . . . . . . . 63
7  Burglary . . . . . . . . . . . . . . . . . . . . . . . . . . . . . . . . . . . . . . . . 96
8  Child Safety . . . . . . . . . . . . . . . . . . . . . . . . . . . . . . . . . . . . 109
9  Elder Abuse . . . . . . . . . . . . . . . . . . . . . . . . . . . . . . . . . . . . 121
10 Office Safety and Workplace Violence . . . . . . . . . . . . . . . . . 129
11 Active Shooter . . . . . . . . . . . . . . . . . . . . . . . . . . . . . . . . . . 135
Conclusion . . . . . . . . . . . . . . . . . . . . . . . . . . . . . . . . . . . . . . . . 141
Acknowledgments . . . . . . . . . . . . . . . . . . . . . . . . . . . . . . . . . . 143
Resources . . . . . . . . . . . . . . . . . . . . . . . . . . . . . . . . . . . . . . . . . 145
Contributors and Experts . . . . . . . . . . . . . . . . . . . . . . . . . . . . . 149

# Foreword

I first met Ron while attending a law enforcement trauma conference. We started talking about policing, and there was an immediate connection. When he told me he was retired, I assumed he started his career in the 1970s. However, through our conversation, I learned that he started the Chicago Police Academy in 1994, when he was forty years old. Ron served honorably until his retirement in 2015. The academy was hard enough for me at age twenty-three, so I cannot imagine going through it at forty. Ron's dedication to pursuing a career with such danger and trauma at that age is one of the many reasons why I respect him so much.

This book on street safety is unlike any other. It is a combination of Ron's experience from many years of service with the Chicago Police Department, as well as detailed research. His explanations on every topic are thorough and easy to understand. Ron's book covers many distinctive facets of safety that the citizens of the United States need today.

The same caring attitude and determination to help law enforcement officers are present in Ron's drive to help the public. I believe the lessons and tools he provides in this book will be as beneficial to the public as the street safety presentations he is known for.

Ron, thank you for trusting me to write the Foreword for such a needed and helpful book. It is my desire that this book will help members of the public learn how to stay safe and that they share these tactics with their family members to help keep them safe as well.

Blessings,
Captain Matthew May
Wake Forest (NC) Police Department

# Introduction

I was a Chicago Police officer for more than twenty-two years and retired on July 15, 2015. I was very fortunate throughout my career, and I had the honor and privilege of being a speaker in the Preventive Programs Unit of the Chicago Police Department for more than thirteen years until it was disbanded in 2010. The Preventive Programs Unit was instrumental in interacting with many community, religious, and business organizations throughout the city. This unit provided presentations on street safety, robbery, burglary, identity theft, senior citizen exploitation, and many other programs to help the public be aware of any potential danger and the likelihood of becoming a victim.

I averaged more than three hundred safety programs a year, and I truly felt that my presentations made a difference in the community. At the beginning of each street safety presentation, my opening comment was, "In the first ten seconds since you first saw me, you've already judged me." I would then ask a member of the audience what they noticed or what stood out to them. I wanted them to describe me as if I were their attacker.

Many individuals in the audience would mention a specific facial feature or the color of the shirt I was wearing. When a large crowd was in attendance, I received a myriad of responses. It was interesting to hear what other people had to say about appearance, personality, and behavior. Some individuals were more perceptive and observant than others. Right after that, I would have a stranger walk into the room, hand me something, and quickly walk out. When asked to describe the stranger, many were baffled and had no clue.

My goal was to have my audience start using their talent for being aware and cognizant of the people around them or those they encountered.

The next message I reinforced was, "It is so important to use good judgment and common sense no matter where you are or the time of day. It is the most important ingredient to staying safe." My next question was, "Would you walk down a dimly lit alley at two a.m. with two guys standing at the end of the alley?" The response was always the same: "*No*, are you crazy?" When I asked why they would not, almost everyone would say it was not a wise choice, especially with the circumstances given.

## FOLLOW YOUR GUT

As individuals and as a society, we are very trusting until something clicks inside us that says, "I am in trouble." Your gut feeling takes over, along with common sense and your survival instinct. No matter what the situation, these instincts will guide you to a safe place. In my opinion, another name for intuition is "gut feeling" or sixth sense. Gut feeling is a voice deep inside our subconscious that warns us of impending danger or that something is not right. Security specialist Gavin DeBecker, in his book *The Gift of Fear*, surmises that everyone has this gift of perception. Gut feeling and perception are "gifts" the subconscious mind ultimately uses to warn a person that danger lies ahead.

A mistake most people make is not trusting their gut feelings, which often proves to have detrimental consequences. You may believe a particular situation or individual is harmless. But at some point in our lives, most of us have made irrational decisions or have been conned into going against common sense or our gut feeling, often because of greed and misplaced trust. I truly believe that 99 percent of the time, a person's gut feeling is correct. *Always trust your instincts!*

Awareness, intuition, and common sense are three unique gifts that we are all blessed with as human beings. A person's gut feeling will ultimately affect how they view every situation they encounter. In my opinion, women are more aware of their surroundings than men. Most women are on guard and often worried about being physically attacked or sexually assaulted. Being

— INTRODUCTION —

threatened is always in the back of their mind, especially if they are alone in a dark and deserted area.

Debbie Pickus, a mental and physical wellness coach for many major companies who has a background in martial arts, related this story about gut feelings.

> A woman I know decided to enjoy a morning walk with her baby and her dog through a wooded area near her home. As she was approaching the woods, her dog was hesitant to proceed, and he whimpered, resisting her attempt to go farther. The dog usually loved this time of day, and his hesitation made no sense. She pulled the dog and forced him to walk with her into the woods. A few feet down the path, she immediately froze in her tracks. She instantly felt something was wrong and feared for her and her baby's safety. The hair on the back of her neck stood erect, her stomach tightened up, and she just knew something wasn't right. She turned and ran home.
>
> The next day, she read in the newspaper about a female jogger who was raped and severely beaten and left for dead in the same woods about the same time she was to begin her walk. She *knew* instinctively that the attacker had been there the day of her walk. The combination of her dog's instincts and the power of her gut feeling (and trusting it) absolutely saved her life.
>
> As I taught in my street safety seminars, with a little practice, anyone can become proficient in the art of perception. I decided to write this book because many of my safety tips can benefit everyone and help them be more aware of their surroundings and possible danger in their daily routine.

I considered my grandmother a wise woman. She would often tell me, "Be careful not to trust everyone. There are a lot of good people in this world, but there is always one person who will try to take advantage; they are salt trying to look like sugar. Don't be deceived by someone who appears to be nice on the outside and evil on the inside. It may take some time, but their true colors will eventually appear."

Every chapter in this book contains actual presentations that I have given throughout my career. I hope my helpful safety suggestions will protect you from harm each and every day.

My motto is "Don't make yourself a victim; be safe, be smart, be prepared." Thank you for taking the time to read my book.

Stay safe!<br>
Dr. Ron Rufo

# –CHAPTER 1–

# STREET SAFETY

*"Safety isn't expensive, it's priceless."*
Jerry Smith

AS A LAW enforcement officer for over twenty-two years, I saw numerous people put themselves in vulnerable situations. We are creatures of habit, and that goes for criminals as well. With the help of extensive reviews of case reports and work with detectives, we can often see a pattern develop and can then position officers to catch offenders before they commit another crime. As officers, we are always aware of the communities we police, and we truly care about the personal safety of all citizens we encounter every day.

"No matter what your status is in life, personal safety and self-care should be foremost in your mind," advises Captain John Doherty of the Chicago Police Department.

> Your personal wealth or lack thereof should matter little when making choices to secure yourself and your personal belongings. Unfortunately, in today's society, people are unable to rely on adequate protection from law enforcement, specifically because of budget cuts and political decisions that have decimated local police and sheriff departments across the country. These include staffing and equipment cuts along with shortages created by

fewer job applicants and the redistribution of assets to do more with less.

With the limited number of officers available to conduct patrol or to respond to cries for help, it's imperative that people avoid sketchy areas and unsavory individuals. Officers on patrol could keep potential criminals at bay, remove them from the area, or stop a criminal from participating in whatever crime they are involved in. However, in the absence of available police, criminals have lost their fear of arrest and know that officers aren't always around, thereby making it easier for them to victimize people.

It is imperative that people realize the limitations of law enforcement, especially now while they are being underfunded and understaffed. People must change their personal safety and security habits to better protect themselves and secure their personal space and property. With that in mind, stay aware, keep informed, walk with confidence and alertness, and frequently check, repair, and replace any weaknesses found within your personal space. No longer can you rely on law enforcement alone; you must be self-reliant and seek the support of the police as necessary.

Eugene Roy, retired chief of detectives for the Chicago Police Department, says,

> The basic responsibility of a police officer is to provide for the safety of the community where he or she works in a manner that is legally sound, ethical, and in conformance with agency policies. But to do so, that officer has to provide for their personal safety as well as that of their fellow officers. Safety is not just physical restraint techniques or tactics. It includes and actually starts with an intellectual, emotional, and spiritual commitment to do the right thing the right way at the right time. Without that type of commitment, officer safety and public safety are compromised.

## MINDFULNESS

A descriptive term for being aware and safe that everyone should take into consideration is mindfulness. *Psychology Today* defines mindfulness as "living in the moment."[1] Mindfulness is being aware and paying attention to everyone and everything we meet. Today, people are constantly in a hurry and always trying to get things done quickly, often with little consideration for their personal safety. Technology is a distraction. Thirty years ago, people were not as distracted as they are today. We are paying more attention to looking at the phone while walking or driving and texting and not paying attention to our surroundings.

Shifting our focus from technology to mindfulness as a means of protection and as a safety mechanism is essential. While technology can play an important role in helping us achieve more physical safety, technology only provides tools. Mindfulness focuses attention from distracting thoughts and actions to being in tune with our surroundings. Mindfulness causes us to use our five senses of sight, sound, smell, taste, and touch. These five senses assist us in enjoying and experiencing the world around us every day, and together, they offer a means of protection and well-being. Individuals who lack any of the five senses often make up for it by enhancing the senses they have.[2]

Debbie Pickus, who we met in the Introduction, was told about being at a conference in a large hotel by a woman who attended one of her trainings. The woman had gone into the ladies' room, secluded and on another floor from all the activity at the conference. When she exited the stall, a large, stocky male immediately grabbed her, wrapping his arms around her shoulders and totally controlling her. She knew he was too powerful to fight off, so she quickly yelled out, "I'm having a heart attack, someone help me!" The offender quickly ran off. Her quick thinking saved her from being hurt. Assailants are typically looking for an easy target. Sometimes it is not fighting an attacker that will save you; it is being aware and using some quick thinking to make yourself a more difficult target.

---

[1] https://www.psychologytoday.com/us/basics/mindfulness
[2] https://neuroscience.stanford.edu/news/supersensors-how-loss-one-sense-impacts-others

## PERSONAL SAFETY AND THE NEED FOR SELF-RELIANCE

Captain John Doherty of the Chicago Police Department says,

> In years gone by, people acted differently. There have long been issues with thieves, thugs, and killers, but there was also some level of humanity among them, and criminals would rarely target women and children. That is far from the actions of criminals today. The availability of immediate news information through round-the-clock television, radio, and social media outlets should give people the understanding that they are extremely vulnerable, that anyone is subject to victimization. From a law enforcement perspective, it is obvious that some people are incapable of perceiving their own vulnerability.

If you look around today, you'll observe a small number of people who easily engage with other people. In days gone by, most people would say hello to nearly anyone passing by. A simple greeting and an act of kindness to help someone carry a bag, pick up a dropped item, open a door, or any number of other personal interactions were the norm, but now people will not or cannot even look other people in the eye. The reasons vary, but some of the inability to look up and be aware of your surroundings is the result of fear. Fear is a difficult human condition to overcome, and it causes people to act in ways they normally wouldn't. Fear fosters prime conditions for becoming a victim.

Retired New York City Police Department (NYPD) Police Sergeant (Special Assignment) Wilem Wong says,

> All individuals need to project situational awareness. Periodically looking away from your smartphone or electronic devices and being aware, looking for potential threats or hazards in your environment, is paramount to your safety. You can tell a lot about an approaching individual. You need to pick up essential cues

and read that person's body language. Make sure there is a safe distance between you and everyone you encounter that can give you more time to react and safely get away.

## AWARENESS AND A WARRIOR MINDSET

Bill Cinkay, a retired police sergeant with the North Riverside, Illinois Police Department, believes people should have a warrior mindset.

> When it comes to safety in everyday life, there is truly only one protection you are guaranteed to have in every single scenario. That defense is more powerful than any weapon, firearm, or explosive. That safeguard is your mind. Why is it more powerful? First, any of the weapons I just mentioned will require the right "mindset" and memories of training to be used effectively. But with awareness, your mind can steer you away from potential danger, thereby avoiding conflict. Also, using visualization, you can mentally prepare for situations that are potentially dangerous, therefore always having a plan.
>
> Violent crime statistics are up in many of our largest US cities, which increases the chances that if you are in the wrong place at the wrong time, you just might be a target or victim of a violent crime. Modern-day criminals have become quite brash when it comes to their victims. Whether you are in a vehicle, a retail establishment, or simply walking down the street, mental preparation is a must because whether you become a target, a victim, or a victor depends on your mindset and ability to pay attention.
>
> When walking, it is important to wear comfortable shoes; an offender will notice the shoes you are wearing. Ladies who wear high heels may be more apt to be attacked because of their inability to run away or chase the offender. A woman wearing high heels is at risk of being pushed off balance, especially from behind. Walking in a well-lit area and having a plan of action is

always wise. A person who thinks ahead and role-plays different adverse scenarios has the advantage of walking away unharmed. Many people who are confronted with a dangerous or frightening situation are often hindered by tunnel vision and have a difficult time recalling specific details.

Many people are clueless when it comes to the possibility of being attacked. Male offenders who demand money from female victims may have another crime on their minds; that crime is *rape*. Does the female seem helpless and unable to fight back? Most male sex offenders are looking for that easy target, the stranded female in the wrong place at the wrong time, or the lone male target who may be drunk and will not put up much resistance. A sex offender will use any means possible to control the situation and get what he wants. There are many circumstances that can lead to a victim getting attacked sexually. The most prevalent are the time of day or night, a deserted or discrete location, and how many people are near the area. The chances of the victim being severely beaten or killed is always a strong possibility, especially if the offender believes their victim can identify them as their attacker to police.

## *Know Your Environment*

Cinkay believes that, first and foremost, knowledge about the areas in which you travel is extremely important.

> We must ask ourselves, *where are the high-crime areas? What specifically are the crimes committed in the areas I am frequenting? Is there a safer route to travel? If I must travel there, what is the safest time of day to be there?* These are just several pieces of information you might want to investigate if either living in or traveling to places that receive media attention about high crime. Once the knowledge is gained, you can then apply awareness upon arrival.
>
> Being aware of your environment is of the utmost importance no matter where you go. Keep your head on a swivel and your nose out of your cell phone. I am baffled when I see anyone just

sauntering down the sidewalk, cell phone in hand, wondering who liked their social media posts. You might as well have a sign on you that says, "I'm not paying attention, please rob me or run me over!" If your attention is focused on anything other than what is going on around you, you are ultimately an easier target.

My advice for everyone is to follow their "gut" or their internal voice. If something does not look right and makes you feel uneasy, it is your ancient instinct kicking in to protect you. Don't ignore this internal voice. It is always better to be safe than sorry.

## *Visualization*

What would you do if a much larger person were to physically attack you? Have you ever thought about it? Have you ever spent time visualizing being grabbed from behind and having to break free to defend yourself?

Cinkay explains the value of visualization.

> Visualization is a powerful tool and is often underrated. Most successful athletes have already played their contests in their minds before they take place, always seeing themselves as victorious. This is a form of practice. If you've already visualized something in your mind numerous times and that event takes place, it won't be foreign to you, making it easier to face the situation if it is challenging. Never—and I mean never—accept defeat mentally in any aspect of your life.
>
> If a physical attack or something else takes place, and escape is not an option, you are now forced to defend yourself. Fear is normal; it creates a burst of biological reactions that provide energy and pain tolerance, and you cannot let fear take total control. Even if you are physically overmatched, you must mentally be prepared to fight for your life with everything you have. Your hands, arms, legs, voice (screaming for help), and teeth are weapons readily available. Offenders of violent crime much prefer a submissive target and are more likely to disengage from someone who is attempting to scratch their eyes out.

Cinkay points out a few vulnerable areas to be aware of if you are attacked and need to defend yourself:
- **Eyes:** They are extremely sensitive to very little contact, and it is difficult to fight if you cannot see.
- **Ears:** It only takes seven pounds of pressure to rip off a human ear.[3]
- **Throat:** A throat strike can cause immediate choking, breathing difficulty, and, if hard enough, even death.
- **Fingers:** It is extremely painful when they are forced into unnatural positions.
- **Groin:** For men, this area is extremely vulnerable, sensitive, and painful when struck.

Keep the above list in mind whether you're being attacked or are on the offensive. A person must have a warrior mindset if they are to survive any violent encounter. Be willing to fight with your entire being to defend yourself. Quitters never win, and winners never quit!

## DISTRACTIONS

Knowing or learning about your surroundings and being aware of who is around you is extremely important to your personal safety. A person is susceptible to attack if they are not paying attention—especially to their surroundings, the area, or the people they encounter. Criminals, who usually work in teams, always bank on distractions to take advantage of any situation and their intended target. Every person should be cautious if there is a fight on the street, a person crying, or someone falling or feigning illness. It is human nature to see what is wrong, perhaps helping if we can, but be cautious of your personal items. You become vulnerable when you are not paying attention, especially if a commotion continues. This is a great way to become a victim, and a thief knows this as well.

Know your location or well-known landmarks in case you do become a crime victim; this will assist the police in getting to the location quickly. There are apps such as LiveSafe that allow a user to send someone their location so

---

[3] https://www.winstonmedical.org/human-ears-and-hearing-facts/

they can be tracked until they reach their destination and then shut off the tracking. Headphones are a great way to listen to music while exercising, jogging, cycling, and doing many outdoor activities, but they make the user more susceptible to an attack.

Captain John Doherty advises,

> Personal safety is as simple as walking with your head up and looking around. Texting, emailing, watching videos, and gathering news have caused people to be struck by vehicles or injured by being inattentive to obstacles in their path. The attention they pay to their portable devices also creates significant security risks, such as not being aware of who is around them, being followed for any number of reasons, and not being able to recognize an oncoming threat. Limiting your time on personal devices while in public will increase your personal security. Thieves grabbing your exposed device, someone following you to a secluded area, or just targeting you for a personal attack can all be avoided by limiting your screen time while mobile in public.

Rev. Dr. Kimberly Lewis-Davis, Chicago Police Department chaplain, says,

> It is important for a person to always be aware of their surroundings, their neighborhood and the sounds, people, and cars nearby. Staying aware can keep you safe. One way is to put the phone away while out and about. It is a distraction. Another way to become more aware is to make mindfulness a daily practice. People are more focused on cell phone messaging or staying connected to technology while walking. Some cell phones are stolen from their owner's hands because of a lack of awareness and not being in the present moment. From a criminal point of view, this is a crime of opportunity because most cell phones are high-ticket items.

## WALKING DOWN THE STREET

Just the way a person walks down the street can determine the likelihood of becoming a victim. It is essential to walk with confidence, appearing to be alert with your head held high. In my opinion, an offender will take between seven and nine seconds to size up a person and decide the right moment to strike. Countless people walk with their heads down, not paying attention to their surroundings. Most likely, they are texting or talking on the phone, and that immediately makes them prime targets.

While walking down the street, we need to keep everyone in our field of vision. Offenders are always watching their victims, seeing if they can take advantage of a person who is not paying attention to their surroundings. A thief will take the path of least resistance and may attack their victim from behind using the element of surprise.

In Chicago and many cities across our nation, alleys are used to get to a garage or as a thoroughfare. My advice for everyone is to be careful if you must walk down an alley; it is best to take the extra time and use a nearby street instead. For the most part, alleys are not well-lit or well-traveled, especially at night. Alleys are full of tall garbage receptacles that a potential criminal can hide behind. Offenders can easily conceal themselves between houses, gangways, neglected garages, or empty lots. A victim who is attacked and hurt can be stranded there for hours, waiting for a passerby to come to their aid.

A criminal looks for weakness when they approach someone for cash, a wallet, or a purse. A victim who resists an offender could be injured or killed if they do so. Give up your property, not yourself. Nothing is worth your life.

Elmwood Park Deputy Chief of Police Andrew J. Hock says,

> It is everyone's responsibility to be alert to things that can happen at any time. In my opinion, crime consists of desire, opportunity, and skill. It is extremely important to use common sense and notice who passes you and who surrounds you. It is not wise to pull up in front of an unknown group of guys and take out packages from your car or run into a coffee shop or gas station with the car running and the keys in the car. Everyone should be

conscious that a person approaching them may commit a crime. If a woman is walking down the street alone and carrying her purse, she needs to be aware of her surroundings. Never flaunt money or jewelry, especially if you are in a crowded room or area. Someone is always watching.

## *Body Language*

When I was young, I often accompanied my grandmother to the bank. I remember her walking into the bank holding her purse at her side. When we came out of the bank, her purse was clenched tightly against her chest. I did not realize it then, but just by her holding her purse in that manner, she might as well have been saying, "Hey, look at me, I have money here." When I mention this story in my safety seminars, everyone laughs as I mimic her body language as she was walking out of the bank. I always finish with the question, "How do you walk when you are carrying money; is it obvious? Remember this story; people will notice."

## HOW TO CARRY A PURSE

How a purse is carried indicates how easily it can be taken. A person's body language says it all. Women who have purses with long straps often carry them with the strap diagonally across the chest. Some safety experts suggest this is a safe way to carry a purse, but I personally disagree. Carrying a purse bandolero-style gives the offender an advantage in controlling the victim by pulling her forward, backward, or even throwing her down by the strap. The strap can also be used to choke the victim or cause her injury.

Women who try to hold onto their purses or fight with the robber often get hurt or eventually fall to the ground as the offender runs away. Offenders have been known to cut purse straps with a sharp knife and sneak into a crowd. I recommend women carry two purses—a small, concealable purse that holds keys, money identification and a larger one for all other necessities. I always recommend not carrying a large amount of cash unnecessarily. Keep your purse close to your body, in front of you, where you can see it, preferably with one hand on top of the flap.

## *A True Story*

Rose Olivieri, a retired Chicago Police officer in the Preventive Programs Unit, relays this true, personal incident.

> My friend, my husband, and I went out to lunch at a restaurant near our home. We walked in and took a seat at a quiet table in the back corner. My friend put her purse on the floor near the corner of the wall. We proceeded to talk, laugh, and enjoy each other's company. When it was time to pay the bill, she reached over to get her purse, but it was not where she had put it. It had been moved. Worried and perplexed, she rifled through her purse and found that all her money and credit cards were gone. She immediately called the credit card company (and was fortunate to remember her credit card number) and was soon told that someone was using her card at a local retail store a few miles away. The police came and said this restaurant and another restaurant nearby were frequently targeted by a group of thieves. The officer said they would often use an umbrella to drag their victims' purses and then leave quickly.
>
> The credit card company was able to stop the many gift card transactions that ensued. With a police report in hand, the victim called all three major credit bureaus and told them about the theft. Her credit line was immediately frozen for fraud. And the restaurant? Management refuses to alert police when this group comes in for fear of retribution, even though they know what is going on.

In all of my safety presentations, I always instructed the many women in my class that they must be aware of who is near them, especially when opening their purses or wallets to pay for an item. They should always try to limit the amount of money and the number of credit cards they carry. With today's electronic means of paying for items, it may be wise to carry only one credit card to make your purchases. I recommend writing down the names of your credit cards, along with account numbers and the 800 numbers for each credit card, and keeping this information in a safe place both at home and in the office. If you are a victim of theft or have lost your purse or wallet, cancel your affected credit cards immediately. Next, file a police report detailing the incident. This will help the owner of the credit card receive credit back for any fraudulent purchases.

At one point in my street safety presentation, to prove a point, I approach a member of my audience and ask for change. I remember one presentation where an older woman with an oversized purse took out her wallet and proceeded to give me change. Her wallet contained about twelve credit cards, a substantial amount of cash, and her social security card, driver's license, and checkbook. A thief would consider this opportunity a bonanza, not only because of the large number of credit cards and the amount of cash but also for the identification and checkbook, all of which increase the likelihood that she will become a victim of identity theft.

I used this woman as a perfect example. I asked her how many credit cards she had, and she said, "I have about nine or ten." There were actually twelve. I asked her to name them, and she could only name about three or four. She had no idea what any of her credit card numbers were nor the 800 numbers to call if she needed to cancel them. If this woman were robbed, by the time she could remember what credit cards she had, find the account numbers, and finally call them in, the offender would have surely maxed out every one of them in her wallet. Usually, the first place an offender uses a stolen credit card is at a gas station to validate that it is good.

## *A Word of Caution about Someone Who Begs for Money*

When someone is begging for money, often their goal is to distract their intended victim so their accomplice can take the victim's wallet or items in their purse. The offender will quickly look for money, credit cards, identification, a passport, checkbook, or other valuable items.

Here is a prime example: A shabbily dressed person approaches a woman on the sidewalk and asks for money. She is a perfect victim because she has packages in her arms and her purse is hanging from her shoulder. He says, "Ma'am, I need help. I need to catch a bus or a train to go see my mom; she is in the hospital." The lady, feeling sorry for the individual, opens her purse and takes out her wallet. Money and credit cards are in plain view. This woman takes out a five-dollar bill and gives it to him. She puts her wallet back into her purse as he nonchalantly touches her shoulder with his hand and asks, "Where do I catch the train?" Touching her shoulder is the signal to his inconspicuous accomplice that this women's wallet is worth taking a chance to steal. With a small coat draped over his forearm, the accomplice quickly reaches into her purse and takes the women's wallet as she is giving directions to catch a train. Both offenders walk away and soon split the money and go shopping with her credit cards, as she is oblivious to what just happened.

As police officers, we often receive calls in the noon hour about a lost or stolen wallet. A woman ready to go to lunch realizes that her wallet is missing from her purse, or a gentleman realizes that his wallet is not in his back pocket. When asked about the last time they saw their wallet, many of the answers are the same: "I had my wallet right before I gave money to that person who looked destitute."

Do not be naïve to the fact that someone is always watching you and what you have. Your intentions may be honorable, but theirs are not. A person who has their wallet taken not only loses their money but has the burden of reporting the crime and replacing the credit cards and other important items taken. Never carry your social security card, passport, birth certificate, or important papers in your purse or wallet unnecessarily.

Another tactic an offender may use is asking a person for the time. Their intention is to see what you have, so be careful. It is my experience that many offenders are drug-addicted and looking for any opportunity to take a watch, phone, or jewelry and trade them for drugs. Women with expensive diamond rings should be aware, especially when walking alone. I recommend hiding the diamond on the inside of the hand and leaving only the band showing.

If you are approached and asked for the time, my advice is to be smart and just guess without showing what you have. Do not pull out an expensive cell phone or show a designer watch on your arm. Either make up a logical-sounding time or do not respond at all and walk away.

If someone threatens you with a gun or a knife and asks for money or your valuables, the most crucial advice I can give that may save your life is this:

*Give up your property, not yourself.*

Most offenders just want their victims' property.

Never go with an offender to another location. This is *vital*. When an offender moves a victim to a different location, their only intention will likely be to harm, sexually assault, or kill their victim.

## *If You're a Victim*

I consider a person's voice a "gift" that they need to use to thwart any attacker. A person who is about to be attacked should scream or yell as loud as they can. If you must fight back to protect yourself, give it your all and do what is best for you. Kick, punch, bite, scratch, and do what you must to get away. Your life may depend on it. Bill Looney, a retired Chicago Police commander of the 16th District, reiterates, "It is important to size up or assess a situation. If a person approaches you with a gun, do not fight, don't resist, just give them what they want, and you will most likely be alive to talk about it."

The time of day is always a factor in a person's safety. Here are two examples, twelve hours apart:

At 2:00 p.m., a person is walking downtown in any city. Rarely will an offender physically attack someone in a crowded area. There will often be many people walking and cars, taxis, and trucks driving by. Perpetrators may fear a Good Samaritan could come to a victim's rescue.

At 2:00 a.m. at the same location: Now everything changes; what a difference twelve hours make. There is minimal pedestrian or vehicular traffic. Now add darkness and lights from street lights. The chances have increased dramatically that anyone walking alone can become a victim of a crime.

## **SHOPPING**

There are many strategies you can use to avoid being attacked while shopping or near a business district. If you feel uncomfortable and suspect you are being followed, do not hesitate to alert the shop owner or one of the store employees. A person is safer in a business establishment that has many employees and customers. It is important not to feel foolish or paranoid about any possible offender in the area. Call 911, or ask someone else nearby to make the call. Gather your thoughts, and give a good and detailed description of the possible offender when the police arrive.

When shopping, always be cautious at the register when you open your wallet to pay. Less is more. Always try to pay with cash if you have a small purchase. Avoid carrying a large amount of cash; other people at the register are often curious, especially if a large amount of cash is displayed. Try to carry just one or two credit cards with you when shopping, and ensure the clerk does not swipe the card twice or use an additional terminal to steal your card information. Keep your receipt, and check your credit card or bank statement.

Offenders tend to target women with numerous bags or with young children as they are browsing a sale rack. Ladies, be careful not to put your purse in a shopping cart or set your shopping bags on the floor when you shop. It does not take long for a thief to move quickly and quietly and take what they can.

Always be aware of potential danger when using public restrooms. I recommend choosing the first or last stall by the wall and keeping your purse, laptop, or personal items in the corner of the stall. This will help avoid anything being taken. Thieves have been known to stand on the toilet and reach over the dividing wall to easily steal a purse hanging on the door hook. The next paragraph explains an incident that happened on my beat.

The loss prevention security team at a major department store was receiving numerous complaints of women having their purses stolen in the store's restrooms. The female thief would go into a stall next to their intended victim. After a minute, the thief would wave her hand underneath the opening at the bottom of the bathroom stall, asking for toilet paper. While the victim was obliging the thief, the thief would stand on the toilet, reach over, and take the victim's purse. The loss prevention detail eventually set up a sting and finally caught the female thief red-handed.

## PARKING LOTS

Never leave valuables visible in your car. Keep anything of value in the trunk. A desperate thief will smash a car window just for loose change. Be cautious of anyone loitering by your vehicle at a mall parking lot or a dark parking lot. I recommend changing parking spaces after shopping, no matter how crowded the parking lot is.

Memorize this simple checklist to reduce your chances of becoming a victim:
- Park in a well-lit space.
- Close the windows and lock the doors.
- Have your keys ready before you approach the car.
- Be cautious if anyone approaches you in a parking lot while you're walking to your car.
- Always lock your car, whether it is parked or you are driving.

## PARKING GARAGES

Be aware of your surroundings when walking through a parking garage. Always watch for someone who is loitering in the area or lurking near your car. Walk quickly to your car with your keys out and ready. If time permits, it is often safer to put your items in the trunk or behind your seat and leave immediately.

Len Cacioppo, a thirty-year Chicago Police veteran, says,

> A hopeful thief will place an empty water bottle or another large object in the rear tire well on the passenger's side of the car. The unsuspecting victim may not notice when they enter the car to drive away. When they begin to move the car, they most likely hear a loud, unfamiliar, crunching noise caused by the bottle or object. Worried about the noise, the victim stops the car to survey what is wrong. The thief will then get into the running car and take off, often with the victim's personal and shopping items intact.
>
> I recommend making a quick walk around your car before getting into it, always keeping your door locked while you are inspecting your vehicle. If you must get out of your car, shut off the engine and lock the doors. Be cautious; if something is not right, do not hesitate to go back into the store and call the police.

If a vehicle or person looks suspicious, try to write down as much information about them as possible. Trying to recall details from memory later is not only difficult but often inaccurate. Jot down the information immediately:

make, model, color; two-door or four-door. Note anything unusual that stands out or is missing from the car. Were there passengers in the car? Never put yourself in jeopardy, and use the safest route to get away.

## PUBLIC TRANSPORTATION

Public transportation is a convenient and efficient means of getting around in many larger US cities. Public transportation on buses and trains is relatively safe, but thieves look for every opportunity to take advantage of any potential victim. Given the abundant number of commuters using public transportation daily, many police departments do not have enough manpower to prevent crime from occurring, especially during the morning and evening commutes when nearly every bus and train is crowded beyond capacity. Thieves are aware of this. Because bus and train rides can become routine and monotonous, commuters soon begin to doze and fall asleep while traveling, and thieves take advantage of the situation. People using a bus or a train should always stay awake and plan the safest route possible.

I have a few suggestions that may keep you safe. Try to sit close to the bus driver or conductor on the train. Try not to sit or stand by the exit door in the back of the bus or train because a thief can take your valuables and run out the back just before the doors close and just before the bus or train departs.

Rose Olivieri, a retired Chicago Police officer specializing in street safety, offers this advice.

> People need to be more aware of their surroundings, especially when riding on public transportation. A passenger should be aware of everyone on the bus or the train they are riding in. Look at the other passengers; size them up; ask yourself if they could be someone you need to keep an eye on. It is important to sit in an aisle seat; this prevents you from being trapped by the window. We have had many reports of theft when the person dozed off and fell asleep; when they woke up, their belongings were gone. Stay awake and alert. Another important tip is to stay as close to the driver as you can. We have responded to many calls where

someone was sitting near the back door of the bus, and a thief grabbed a lady's purse, wallet, or jewelry as they ran off the bus. This is where they may work in teams because someone will block the person from getting off the bus to chase the thief. Do not count your money or open your wallet for any reason; a thief will take advantage of this type of situation. My last piece of advice is this: do not look like a victim. Be confident and look like you are not a person that can be taken advantage of.

Lynne Ansani, a lifelong Chicago area resident, shares this story.

On an early Chicago morning commute into the city, the train had the usual assortment of people, most keeping their heads down, staring intently at their phones and not paying attention to their surroundings. A man about fifty years old, shabbily dressed, nonchalantly lit a cigarette on the train. Almost immediately, a man sitting by the door spoke out loudly, "Hey, you can't smoke on the train." That was the last comprehensive sentence I heard for a while as they continued to argue back and forth. The argument became heated and escalated quickly as the train pulled away. I looked around at my fellow passengers, and they were either staring at their phones or staring out the window. No one was getting involved. The tone of the argument was very disturbing to hear and witness as I began to wonder if either of these guys had a gun. We were stuck on a moving train with no place to go. I dialed 911 and told the dispatcher what was happening, and gave the train number and station we were about to head into. I then texted my sister and my best friend and told them what was happening. As the train pulled into the station, everyone ran out, and soon after, four Chicago Police officers ran in and took both men off the train. One officer found a gun on the man who was smoking.

Going to work that day could have been disastrous. I was upset and nervous all day until I got home safely that evening and hugged my two sons. I was so thankful that I was not a statistic on the evening news. That incident taught me to be more aware of my surroundings no matter where I am.

Retired NYPD Police Sergeant (Special Assignment) Wilem Wong says many crimes on the transit system are crimes of opportunity. He estimates that in 2012, 5 million riders used approximately 475 subway stations in their daily commute within New York City (not including Staten Island). He noticed a significant number of larcenies of cell phones—especially iPhones—when he worked in the NYPD Transit Bureau in the Bronx and Queens from 2012 to 2014.

At the time he patrolled the subways, many people were not very aware of their surroundings. Many commuters owned Apple's iPhone 4 or 5 and seemed to be mesmerized by them. Thieves often grabbed a victim's phone right before the subway doors would close. The term "apple picking" was often used to refer to any thief who committed this brazen crime. Sgt. Wong says that when a seasoned criminal is caught with a phone, he will claim that it is his phone that was stolen, and everything must be sorted out at the precinct.

Wong says most crimes that occur on public transportation in New York are harassment, intimidation, threatening behavior, fighting, gang and gun violence, pickpockets, and con games. He advises commuters to

- be cautious of anyone who comes into your personal space, especially if the thief nudges you on a crowded bus or train;
- remain in a well-lit area, and observe the behavior of those around you. If you feel uneasy or threatened, change your seat, and alert the conductor or driver if possible;
- avoid wearing expensive-looking watches, rings, chains, or necklaces. Whenever possible, remove or cover up chains and rings, or turn a ring where a diamond or stone is facing inward toward the palm of the hand so it cannot be seen; and
- try *not* to sit in the back of the bus, especially by the back door. Most thieves have accomplices who help them get away easily.

## *A Card Scam Often Played on Public Transportation*

A confidence game called Three-Card Monte is often played on buses and trains, near bus stops and on train platforms, and near busy tourist and shopping areas. It is a street game that entices the curious victim, often known as a "mark," to get in on the action. Many of the participants who are playing the game are in on the con. They are great actors being loud, laughing, and high-fiving each other as they enjoy the money they are supposedly winning. The victim, curious to know what all the excitement is about, gets closer to joining in the game. Greed and the excitement to win money take over. The dealer of Three-Card Monte has the hands of a magician, and the victim will be chasing their money and will never win.

I have seen this game firsthand, coming off a cruise ship in a small port. A police officer happened to approach, and all the con artists walked away, the dealer included, leaving the dumbfounded passengers trying to get their money back. All the crooks eagerly returned when the police officer was out of sight, and a new game began all over again.

## BEING SAFE IN TRAFFIC

Drivers at a stoplight should always be aware of their immediate surroundings. A driver approaching a stoplight should stay at least one car length away from the vehicle ahead of them. They should ensure that the back wheels of the car in front of them are in plain view so they can drive away if they need to. It is important for a driver to never get boxed in between two cars, and always keep a safe distance to escape if a threat occurs. When someone is begging for money at a stoplight, stay back until that person either passes or you can proceed promptly when the light turns green.

Always know the area you are in and the best way to leave quickly. Always look around when entering your vehicle, and have your keys out and ready. Lock your doors immediately upon entering your vehicle, and keep the doors locked and your windows rolled up. And finally, never exit your vehicle while the car is running.

Rose Olivieri, a retired Chicago Police officer in the Preventive Programs Unit, shares this story.

> My niece was driving home late from work one evening, and she was by herself. The car in front of her had no plates, and there

appeared to be at least four individuals in the car. She stayed a safe distance behind them, but her suspicions grew. At the next stoplight, near a cemetery, four males jumped out of the car and headed back toward her car. She immediately hit the gas, swerved around them, and sped away. Her instincts were right on; she did the right thing and was aware of what could have occurred.

I suggest the following:
- By texting and driving, a driver is at higher risk of an accident by just looking down for a few seconds. If you need to use the phone, find a safe place to pull over.
- Don't open your car window more than one inch to speak to someone approaching your car. Drive away immediately if you feel uncomfortable.
- If you suspect another car is following yours, do not go home. It is best to drive to the nearest police or fire station or a brightly lit convenience store and stay in your car. Call 911 from your cell, and know your location. Stay in your car, and honk the horn repeatedly in short blasts until someone comes to help.

## RANDOM ACTS OF VIOLENCE

Captain John Doherty of the Chicago Police Department says,

> The victimization of people from nearly every walk of life is increasing exponentially, facts that are shown daily in reports of street robberies, carjackings, burglary, theft, and random shootings. Although no shooting is truly random, most people who are not specifically targeted during a shooting incident are injured as a result of errant gunfire. Someone else may be targeted for any number of reasons, but the fired bullets miss their target, resulting in gunshot injuries to otherwise-innocent bystanders. Whether you are intentionally victimized by robbery at gunpoint or knifepoint, your home or vehicle is burglarized for the property inside, or

you're injured in your daily routine through the negligent actions of others during a violent attack, it is paramount to realize you need to be prepared to act to protect yourself, your children or family, or another innocent person being similarly victimized.

# CARJACKINGS

Many large cities have been experiencing daily carjackings. It is important to avoid being alone, especially at night and especially in high-crime areas. Get in the habit of keeping your cell phone in your pocket just in case your car is taken so you will have a chance to call 911 for help. Anyone who is a victim of a crime should report the crime immediately so details will be fresh in their memory.

If you are a victim of a carjacking, it is important to stay calm, give up your car, and try to get a good description of the offenders. It is essential to avoid parking by dumpsters, isolated areas, large trucks, vans, or obstacles that may limit visibility. Carjackings often occur at gas stations, intersections, convenience stores, parking lots, automatic teller machine (ATM) locations, and desolate areas.

Rose Olivieri agrees.

> We have experienced a tremendous increase in carjackings. These offenders look for a vulnerable victim driving a nice or expensive car. Carjackers have been known to grab the victim's keys and cell phone. My recommendation is to carry a dummy phone and a spare set of bogus car keys, especially if you have a newer car with push-button ignition. That way, once they shut off the engine, the car will not start without your real ignition key.

Carjackings can occur at any time, but they happen most often under cover of darkness. Carjacking offenders have been known to lightly tap a car at a stoplight. As the driver exits their car to inspect the damage to their vehicle, someone jumps into the empty car and drives away. Be careful of stranded motorists, and always avoid driving alone.

Lt. Frank Scarpa of the Richmond Virginia Police Department tells the following story.

> I was a new sergeant assigned to the Second Precinct. One night on the graveyard shift on the southside of Richmond, a call came out of a robbery and carjacking in progress at a 7-11 near a large housing complex. Two men on their way to work stopped at the 7-11 to get a cup of coffee. They said they both noticed a guy hanging around the convenience store but thought nothing of it. What they did not know was that this guy had a plan, and he had been waiting for the right opportunity to isolate a victim when no one else was in the parking lot. Unfortunately for these two gentlemen, they walked out to their car when no one else was around, giving the suspect just enough time to point a gun at them, take their wallets, and take off in their car. After a short vehicle and foot chase, the perpetrator was arrested and positively identified in the police lineup. The victim's property was recovered, and thankfully, no one got hurt. My best advice is always to be aware of your surroundings and keep your head on a swivel, but if you are approached, just give the criminal want they want; it is not worth your life.

Lt. Scarpa also relayed another story about carjacking.

> A young woman walked out of a grocery store that was notorious for drug dealing, prostitution, and other criminal activities. She was walking to her car when two young thugs put a gun to the back of her waist and demanded the keys to her car. They quickly took off in her car, but unbeknownst to them, this vehicle was equipped with ONSTAR. One quick phone call to 911 and our communication officers were already receiving the location of the stolen vehicle. Officers soon spotted the car and tried to pull it over. A pursuit began through residential neighborhoods and alleys. Because of the danger and the offenders' reckless driving,

the pursuit was called off, but ONSTAR continued to track the vehicle. The offenders soon abandoned the car and got away. The victim was able to get her car back. My advice, if you can afford it, is to add ONSTAR to your car. Never challenge a robber or carjacker; just give them your property or vehicle.

Lt. Adrienne Gardner of the Richmond, Virginia, Police Department agrees that carjackings are on the rise across the country and continue to occur in her jurisdiction with some frequency.

Many of our robbery and stolen-vehicle offenders victimize local pizza and fast-food delivery drivers. They also target Door Dash and Uber Eats drivers and people who think that they are going to run into a store "for just a minute" to pick up a to-go order. When it comes to carjackings, offenders have been known to place orders to be delivered to false or vacant addresses. When the delivery person arrives, the offenders take the food, take the driver's money and personal items, and speed off in their car. My advice is to be vigilant about who is near you when you exit your vehicle; always look at your rearview and side mirrors.

Shockingly, I recall several incidents in the past few years in my department where cars were stolen with children inside of them. Each incident involved someone who was at a convenience store or picking up a take-out food order, and they left their young child (often an infant) in the car while they ran into the store. In mere seconds, the offenders entered the unlocked and running vehicle and drove away. I'm certain the offenders were surprised to find the children inside, often ditching the car immediately with the child still inside. Thieves look for any opportunity to take a car that is left unattended with the victim's keys inside, a costly mistake that can be avoided by taking the necessary precautions. If confronted, give up whatever the assailant asks for so as to not escalate a property crime into a violent crime.

## THEFT FROM A VEHICLE

Theft from an auto is a crime of opportunity, and all break-ins have one thing in common: something was left in the car worth stealing. It is common for most people to leave items in their cars. Even items that may not have much monetary value may be worth something to a thief. Avoid leaving packages or shopping bags out in the open. A thief will break into a car if they see anything of value in plain sight, even a few coins.

It is important to always lock all vehicle doors. This is true even if you will be away "for just a second." Thieves look for easy targets. Remember that it only takes a short time to steal something from your car. Thieves walk down neighborhood streets and rows of cars in car parking lots, checking for unlocked doors or open windows. An offender will break a $200 car window just to steal change.

Very few break-ins are random. Take your valuables with you or keep them in the trunk. Park in a busy area that has a lot of activity. Thieves prefer isolated areas where they can steal practically unnoticed. Car alarms and antitheft devices most often act as a deterrent, but a thief may still attempt to break into your vehicle. Here are additional tips for keeping items safe inside your car:

- Keep the ignition key separate from your home keys.
- Leave only an ignition key with a valet or parking attendant.
- Do not hide a spare key under the floor mat or under the hood.
- If possible, avoid parking on the street, and try to park in areas that are locked or have an attendant on-site.

## TAXI CABS

Riding in taxis can be safer than using public transportation, and most taxi drivers know the quickest route to a person's destination. There were a number of times when, as a police officer, I was stopped by visitors from out of town who had left personal items in the taxi after they exited the vehicle. When asked about the color of the cab, the name, or the cab number, many did not remember. Trying to retrieve an important item from a taxi may become exhausting and fruitless without the important information needed to get it back. I suggest you always take note of the cab number and its color and name. When exiting a cab, always look back to see if you left anything behind.

## VACATIONS

Many travelers are often unaware that their names and addresses are attached to their luggage. I am sure not many people realize the number of people who come in contact with their luggage before they even board a plane. The taxi, limo, LYFT or Uber driver, the porter and other airline personnel at the airport, and the TSA screener all have the opportunity to jot down a person's information and pass it along to anyone who is interested. I recommend that everyone use their work address and their cell phone number on their luggage.

Social media is a great platform that many thieves use to find out who is away from their residence on vacation. It amazes me how many naïve people send pictures in real time from their vacation destination. This gives a burglar ample time to not only stake out the property but take their time burglarizing the home. I also recommend being cautious about who you tell that you are going on vacation, especially in public. I suggest asking a trusted friend or neighbor to check on your property every few days, collecting the mail and newspapers to ensure your residence looks lived in. Filling up the garbage and putting out their garbage on trash day will give the appearance the home is occupied. If a person uses a recording at work, it is important to say that you will be out of the office in meetings but still in town. Never unknowingly give a burglar any added information; protect your investment.

## TRAVELING TO ANOTHER CITY

When an individual visits another city, state, or country, the likelihood of them standing out among the local citizens is inevitable. A person often stands out by the way they are dressed or by their speech. Just by saying a few words, they may indicate that they are new and unfamiliar with the area. Thieves know this, and they use the person's unfamiliarity with their surroundings to their own advantage. Tourists carry cameras and maps and often ask for directions. I recommend that when visiting another city, read up on the attractions and places of interest you would like to visit ahead of time. Knowing where you are going and how to get there safely should be a major consideration. The front desk or hotel concierge can instruct you on the safest route and what to look out for. Thinking ahead will minimize your risk. Try to only keep a few credit cards with you, and use the same one as much as possible. Always keep a watchful eye when paying your bill because it is easier to take advantage of an unsuspecting tourist.

Captain John Doherty of the Chicago Police Department advises,

> Pickpocketing, thefts from rental cars, and thefts from hotel rooms are crimes quite prevalent in areas frequented by tourists and vacationers. As a matter of habit, valuables like wallets, cash, cameras, laptops, and tablet computers should always be secured—never leave them in cars or out in the open in hotel rooms. They are easily taken and are hot items targeted by thieves.

## *Conventions*

If you are attending a convention in an unfamiliar city, it is important not to wear indicators or ID tags that you are a guest at the convention center. Thieves know that a large majority of conventioneers are from out of town. As one, you make a perfect target, especially while wandering outside the convention area. A concierge at a hotel is very knowledgeable about the area and how safe it is. A nearby tourist attraction may be safe, but getting there may be dangerous. Definitely do not consult a map while you're out in public because it is an obvious indicator that you are unsure of where you are going.

Ken Grandy, a retired Chicago Police detective and the retired director of security for Hyatt Regency Corporation, McCormick Place in Chicago, warns against letting your guard down too much while on vacation or at a convention. He says,

> I have seen women leave unattended drinks at the bar to dance and then come back to their drink. My recommendation is to keep your drink with you at all times. If you forget your drink at

the bar, dispose of it immediately. Don't take a chance because it is easy for someone to spike an unattended drink. I recall a situation with a forty-year-old female executive who left her drink at the bar to dance. She was later seen roaming the halls of the hotel, dazed, naked, and confused, but not drunk. Her drink was obliviously tampered with.

## HOTEL SAFETY

Ken Grandy advises that when going into your room, you should "double lock your doors once inside. Also, be sure you pull the door shut when you leave because, occasionally, your hotel door will not completely shut. Offenders have been known to walk the halls of hotels looking for doors that are slightly ajar."

### *Front Desk*
I recommend always keeping track of your luggage when you are checking in at the front desk. Anyone can easily walk away with them when you are busy with the hotel clerk. Keep bags in front of you if possible. Be cautious when giving out information about your hotel room number or personal information; you never know who is listening.

### *Which Floor to Stay On*
A hotel or motel room is not 100 percent safe. I recommend not staying on the first floor because of a greater possibility of an easier break-in. Instead, try to stay in any room between the second and fifth floors. In case of fire, it is easier to access the stairs and get out safely.

### *Emergency Exits*
Check the locations of the emergency exits and where the fire extinguishers are located. A friend of mine who is a former flight attendant suggests counting the number of doors between your room and the emergency stairs on your floor so that in the event a fire fills the hallway with smoke, you will know how far to crawl below the smoke to safety.

### Staying in Your Room
When going to bed, ensure that your door is locked with the deadbolt secure. Never answer your door to an unexpected visitor. If one appears at your door, and you are worried or scared, call the front desk and speak to security.

### Room Safes
Many hotel rooms are equipped with smaller safes. Use them with caution. Management has a master key that will open any safe in case of emergency, but put that key in the wrong hands and valuables can be taken easily. It is important to always know how much money and which valuables you placed in them. These safes often need a four-digit code to gain entry. Make the combination of numbers easy to remember, but do not use 1234 or any four consecutive numbers like 1111. The most important advice I can give is to limit the amount of jewelry taken on a trip. Keep your cash in a few different articles of clothing, such as inside socks or shoes. If some money is taken, at least all of it will not be lost.

### Hotel Wi-Fi
Almost every hotel offers free Wi-Fi to their customers. This service is often an unprotected public internet that anyone can access. Your personal and private information can be easily compromised by a thief who takes control by gaining access to your username and password from your phone, tablet, or laptop computer.

### Meet the Housekeeper
I recommend taking the time to meet the housekeeper who will be servicing your room, so they associate you with your room number. This reduces the chances of them allowing someone into your room when it is being serviced. I also recommend that you keep your room and personal items neat and orderly, so you will recognize if something is out of place upon your return.

### When Out of Your Room
Leave the DO NOT DISTURB sign on your door and the TV on low when you are out of the room. This will give the impression that you are in the room.

## *In Case of a Personal Emergency*

In the last week of my police career, I was assigned a call to assist the Chicago Fire Department at a hotel on my beat downtown. I arrived at the same time the ambulance crew was going up the elevator. An overweight man had collapsed on the floor, and his wife was crying in disbelief. She told us she and her husband were from Texas, and he had just received a new knee that morning. He was fine until he went to get a glass of water, and then he collapsed.

The woman said she dialed 911 on the hotel phone, but instead of being connected to the City of Chicago's 911 emergency system, she was transferred to a department within the hotel. She frantically tried again, thinking she had dialed the wrong number in her nervousness, but she reached the same department in the hotel. She finally called the hotel desk clerk on duty, who dialed 911 for her.

The ambulance team performed CPR until they arrived at the hospital, and the man's wife cried hysterically, blaming herself for not getting the necessary help for her husband sooner. Sadly, the gentleman passed away at the hospital.

The important lesson was that at this hotel, she needed to dial 9 to get an outside line and then 911 for any emergency. Always know how to call in an emergency. Make sure 911 will get you to the police, fire, or paramedics when you call. Some hotels and motels still require you to dial another number to get an outside line before you can call 911. Most hotels have now upgraded their systems to ensure that their guests can get help immediately if they dial 911 on their room phones.

Here are a few additional hotel safety tips:
- Make sure your reservations are guaranteed if you are arriving late.
- Do not enter the room if you suspect someone is in it or if you are being followed, or if someone is lingering near your door.
- Leave instructions with the front desk and others in your party not to give out your room number or your name.
- Check your room phone to ensure it is working properly. If you are in a motel, try to get a room next to the office or the manager's unit.
- Ensure all windows and doors are locked at all times, especially if you are out of your room.

## REVOLVING DOORS

Revolving doors at a store, hotel, or office can be used as a trap to take your valuables if you are not paying attention. Thieves often target women with children and women carrying many shopping bags while entering a revolving door. It takes two thieves for this crime to happen. One thief will intentionally walk ahead of the person who intends to use the revolving door. The thief will pretend to drop something, stopping the door and trapping the victim with just enough space for the second thief to put their hand through the opening to grab the victim's purse, laptop, bags, or briefcase.

But there are ways to lessen your chances of becoming a victim of this type of crime:

- Do not be in a hurry to enter a revolving door; make sure no one is going through it ahead of you.
- Ensure the path is clear to enter and exit the revolving door freely.
- Because this is considered a "right-handed" crime, carry your belongings on your left side.

## ELEVATORS

Most people take elevators for granted, feel safe, and do not believe they may become a victim in one, but elevators can be dangerous if you are not alert. Being in a small and crowded space for a short period of time can be an ideal place for a thief to strike.

If possible, and if time allows, try to enter an empty elevator.

If you are entering the elevator at the lobby or lower level, and someone is already inside but does not exit the elevator at the lobby or lower level, don't get in. Make an excuse if you have to, and wait for another elevator. When entering an elevator, go directly to the control panel and try to stay as close to it as possible. Try not to get trapped in the back of the elevator.

If you are worried or feel threatened by someone in the elevator, press every button for each floor, get off on a floor where you feel safe or where people may be congregating that can help you. A lobby of a building is typically a safe bet because it often has people in the area. Many elevators have alarms if something goes wrong, but be aware that some older elevators stop when the alarm button is pressed.

## *Self-Defense*

Next, I would like to share some tips for protecting yourself in any location or situation.

I highly recommend self-defense classes. They will help you become more confident in your ability to protect yourself if you are confronted by someone who wants to harm you. An offender is banking on the element of surprise, so self-defense training prepares you to always be more aware.

How you respond to an attacker is important. Learning how to use a strong, loud, and offensive yell, along with directed punches and kicks that will scare most offenders away, is the goal of self-defense training.

Simple items like a ballpoint pen can be used as a weapon. A pen or a knife can be easily concealed and be an effective weapon if used properly. Most offenders are *not* expecting their victims to fight back. My suggestion is always to go for the eyes, throat, or groin. If an offender attacks, use the pen or knife on their inner thigh or genital area. This is most often their weakest area. The art of self-defense teaches fighting techniques that are likely to keep a victim safe from harm.

## *Pepper Spray*

I was fortunate to speak at a police training conference in St. Louis, Missouri, in March of 2022. We had an excellent opportunity to attend an interesting seminar at Security Equipment Corporation, one of the leading companies that manufacture SABRE pepper spray products. On the tour of their plant and facility, we learned the intricate details of how pepper spray is manufactured. Their standard of quality is amazing, and they are dedicated in their efforts to make their pepper spray the best product on the market. SABRE has "an industry exclusive high-performance liquid chromatography (HPLC) laboratory that guarantees its maximum strength formulation in every canister to help give you the peace of mind, certainty, reliability, and safety"[4] you want and expect, especially when you need it most.

---

[4] https://www.sabrered.com/pepper-spray-frequently-asked-questions

I recommend anyone carrying pepper spray should have it ready to use when walking, especially if alone. A person's eyes are extremely sensitive, and pepper spray is a legal deterrent to stop any offender(s) from causing harm. In any attack, your main goal is to get away quickly and safely.

> I endorse SABRE's pepper spray products. Their safety products can be trusted to work efficiently and are tested often to discourage anyone from doing harm or injury to a likely victim. The company says these are the top five reasons to carry pepper spray:
> 1. Pepper spray offers protection at a safe distance. Why go hands-on with an attacker if it isn't necessary?
> 2. It offers practical protection against multiple threats.
> 3. It is convenient and practical to use. Pepper spray is legal to carry in all fifty states.
> 4. It is ideal for everyone, and it is easy to carry and conceal. It doesn't require size or strength to use.
> 5. It is proven as an effective and valuable item that can help to stop the most aggressive offender. Police officers throughout the world carry pepper spray.

All safety products should be used with extreme caution. It is important to always follow any manufacturer's instructions when using their safety products. There is no safety product that can guarantee a person's safety in the event of an attack. It is important to realize that failure to properly use a safety product can result in the inability to stop an attacker. Always be ready to take other countermeasures if necessary.

David Nance, a personal safety expert and CEO of Security Equipment Corporation (manufacturer of premium SABRE pepper spray products), says,

> It is important to choose the right pepper spray and look for the maximum strength formula that suits your needs. I recommend

you consider the number of shots a pepper spray container has for the best protection in case you should find yourself needing to defend against multiple threats.

Citizens today are the most distracted they have ever been, especially staring at their phones while walking or at a stoplight, which is the most common mistake people make. Make yourself a difficult target, and walk with your shoulders back and your head and chin up. A person walking with confidence may come off as a more intimidating presence, and they may scare off a potential threat with their body language alone. That may not always work, and that is where pepper spray can make a difference.

## *Personal Alarms*

Personal alarms can be another tool for keeping safe. Most criminals do not want confrontation and can be scared off or frightened away by any resistance, opposition, or struggle. The loud, high-pitched, and obnoxious sound from a personal safety device can be a powerful deterrent in many ways. It can prevent an attack from occurring, or it may attract other people in the area to react to someone in distress, causing the attacker to flee. The attacker does not want to be identified, and personal alarms create witnesses out of those in the immediate area.

In addition to making pepper spray, Security Equipment Corporation also manufactures security devices, including personal alarms. CEO David Nance says,

> Not everyone is completely comfortable using pepper spray or stun guns for self-defense, or users might be younger and need an age-appropriate option. Fortunately, there still are ways to better protect yourself without confronting an attacker directly. Personal alarms can give a person an extra layer of safety in warding off attackers and summoning help when they need it. We have a wide range of personal safety alarms that are easy to carry and feature a dual-siren construction that enables our alarms to be heard from one thousand feet away.

Personal alarms from SABRE are highly portable. Many of them are no larger than the electronic key fob used to unlock car doors, making them easy to attach to a purse, key ring, or backpack. Activating a personal alarm is easy; simply push the button or pull the ring to sound the alarm. The convenience and ease of use of these alarms make them a great choice for anyone in need of extra protection. Because they do not require aim or focus, they can be used by people with disabilities, children, teenagers, and senior citizens.

Many law enforcement professionals recommend using a personal alarm because it can be very effective in warding off threats. Some states have restrictions on other types of safety products like pepper spray or stun guns. This means personal safety alarms may be one of the best legal options available to you for keeping yourself safe. A person may be restricted from traveling with pepper spray products (pepper spray must be stored in your checked luggage only on airplanes), so in some instances, alarms could be the best choice for protection when you are on the road and on flights. When your safety is threatened, seconds matter. Our alarms can activate in an instant, giving you the time to make your escape or get help.

## *Stun Guns*

Stun guns are another personal safety option that is nonlethal and does not require a license to carry. Stun guns work by instantaneously emitting electrical shocks to immobilize and disorient the would-be assailant. Carrying a stun gun may buy you a critical moment in the event of an attack. Who can possess a stun gun varies by state, sometimes even from county to county. Stun guns are legal in most states, but like pepper spray, they require the user to be at least eighteen years old without a felony record, and they can only be used for self-defense. Most states where stun guns are permitted do not require a permit, training, or classes to carry, and they allow the owner to have them in plain view in public. A few states allow stun guns only under special conditions. There are also several countries that completely outlaw stun guns.

Stun guns really do not look like real guns at all and are only effective for immobilizing an attacker if standing close enough to hold the device against the attacker's body.

David Nance says,

> Regardless of your profession, your neighborhood, or your daily routine, personal security should always be important to you and your family. Stun guns are increasingly seen as a practical means of self-defense because they are fairly compact and provide an intimidating deterrent. A person armed with the right self-defense equipment, along with the knowledge and preparation to use it properly, may effectively escape an attacker without the risk of delivering a lethal blow. Men, women, security workers, property owners, and virtually anyone with the right preparation can use stun guns as a self-defense tool.
>
> It is important to remember you do need to make direct contact with the attacker for the stun gun to be effective. Be ready to move away quickly after making contact, as the deterring effects are short-lived. Nonetheless, if the stun gun is your product of choice, it can be a very effective deterrent device.

## – CHAPTER 2 –

# How to Describe a Person

*"He had a thick moustache, and his eyes peered out from his long, lank black greasy hair, like a light from a cinema screen before the drab velvet curtains had been fully withdrawn."*
Jim Lowe, New Reform

DESCRIBING A PERSON is not as easy as you might think. Even when ten people see the same person, there may be ten different descriptions.

A victim may only have a few seconds of contact with their offender, and the combination of surprise and disbelief may be factors that keep you from getting a good description.

Here are a few questions you can ask yourself quickly:
- Is he/she younger or older than I am?
- Is he/she taller or shorter than I am?
- Does he/she weigh more or less than I do?

When doing my presentations, I would often ask the people who attended my safety seminar to describe me in detail. I do this about fifteen minutes into my presentation, plenty of time for them to get an accurate description. These are the questions I asked my audience:
1. What is my age?
2. What is my height?

3. What is my weight?
4. What is the color of my eyes?
5. What is the color of my hair? Can you describe it?
6. What am I wearing?
7. I have two distinguishing facial features; what are they?
8. Am I right-handed or left-handed?
9. What is my nationality?
10. Am I wearing any jewelry?

## CLOTHING

If I ask five witnesses to describe an accident that just occurred, I am sure I will get a few similarities and probably many different insights into what happened. Most people will describe someone from top to bottom. A few people may describe in great detail a person's facial features, the clothes they are wearing, and other important details, while others will have no clue and cannot assist in any kind of description, and the rest of us will fall somewhere in between.

One of the most important things the police need to apprehend an offender(s) is a good description, and as I say in my presentations, one of the most important details is what someone is wearing from the waist down. Any offender who commits a crime can easily take off their shirt, jacket, or outer garment and dispose of these when trying to get away. The offender can also put on an outer garment or something to alter their appearance. But as Bill Looney, a retired Chicago Police commander of the 16th District, says, "When sizing up someone, look at their shoes . . . they are not taking them off." An offender will rarely take off their pants or shoes when trying to get away. Remembering this will really be important in apprehending the offender.

Describing a person's appearance is not an easy task. To be proficient, you have to practice. Being able to describe someone comes naturally for some people, while others will struggle with remembering what they saw, especially if they were attacked. When a person is nervous, they will often experience "tunnel vision" and not really remember too much. An encounter with an offender may only last a few seconds; how descriptive can a victim be?

## An Experience with Description

One day, while working the afternoon shift in the Bridgeport area in the 9th District in Chicago, my partner and I got a call about a robbery that had just occurred. We went to the location with lights and a siren. The victim, an elderly blind woman, was standing on the sidewalk, crying as we pulled up. Yet she was able to give us one of the best descriptions of her attacker I have received to this day because she was in tune with her other senses. She told us in detail about her attacker taking her purse. She described him as a male Hispanic with a raspy voice and about five foot seven inches, similar in height to her son. She said his jacket was a silky, nylon-type windbreaker. He told her he had a gun. She amazed me when she said, "My attacker had on the same cologne as my son; he was wearing Old Spice cologne." I was shocked by how aware this older blind woman was and how well she described her attacker. We toured the area, but we were unable to locate anyone matching her description of her attacker.

A few hours later, my partner and I walked into a fast-food place a few blocks from where the robbery occurred. The place was crowded, and a Hispanic gentleman was at the counter ordering a sandwich. I heard a distinctly rough and raspy voice when he placed his order. My ears perked up as I nudged my partner to listen. He spoke broken English, and he was wearing a yellow windbreaker. He turned and spotted us and then quickly left through the side door with his order. We immediately followed him, and he began to run toward a park across the street. We were able to get him after he stumbled and fell. Lifting him up, I smelled the scent of Old Spice cologne. We cuffed him for our protection and called one of our Spanish-speaking officers. After a brief interview with the Spanish-speaking officer, we took our suspect back to the crime scene to possibly get a positive voice ID from the female victim. In front of her, the Spanish-speaking officer asked the alleged offender, "Where do you live?" He mumbled an address close by, and the blind woman immediately said, "That's him!"

After the positive voice ID, the offender was placed under arrest for armed robbery. The Spanish-speaking officer read him his Miranda rights in Spanish and took him to the station for processing, where we

> learned he had numerous prior convictions for armed robbery. At the court hearing, the defense attorney did his best to squash the victim's descriptive testimony because she was blind. The judge praised the blind woman for her courage and her outstanding description. The judge found the offender guilty and charged him with additional time because she was a disabled senior citizen.
>
> If this lady who was blind can give a great description, you can too.

## COMPARE YOUR DESCRIPTION TO SOMEONE YOU KNOW

One recommendation I have is to compare the person you are describing to someone you know. For example, in one of my presentations, a woman said I reminded her of her brother-in-law. Here are a few descriptive examples and synonyms for those descriptors:

**Height:** "He is about Bob's height, about six feet tall." Other descriptive words for height include short, tall, lanky.

**Weight:** "She is about Vanessa's weight, probably 120 to 125 pounds." Other descriptive words for weight include thin, petite, obese, pot-bellied, overweight, heavy, well-built.

**Age:** "He looks like Jim, and he just retired. Maybe sixty-three to sixty-five years old." Try to give a two- to three-year range if possible. Other descriptive words for age include young, old, preteen, adolescent, teenager, in their twenties, middle-aged, senior citizen.

## DESCRIPTIVE FEATURES

A number of descriptive words can be used to describe someone. Below is a partial list of options:

- **Skin color and tone:** white, Black, olive, light-skinned or dark-skinned, sallow (yellow or pale brown), tanned; and each color has various shades

- **Hair:** thick, thin, curly, long, medium, wavy, short, crewcut, balding or bald, spikey, unkept, weave, plugs, dreadlocks, toupee, or hairpiece
- **Hair color:** black, brown, brunette, blond, red, gray, auburn, copper, white, highlights, partially gray, silver multicolored, bold roots, shiny, or greasy looking
- **Cheeks:** rosy, high cheekbones, chiseled cheekbones
- **Chin:** double, squared, prominent or long, cleft
- **Mouth/lips:** thin, thick, missing teeth, braces
- **Nose:** long, narrow, lopsided, fleshy, red, curved, Roman or Grecian (large), prominent, pug
- **Ears:** oversized, small, pointed, with earrings, with piercings, attached earlobes
- **Forehead:** high, short, wrinkled, balding, smooth, narrow, or prominent
- **Eyebrows:** thick, thin, bushy, arched
- **Eyes:** round, slanted, oval, almond-shaped, hooded, bulging
- **Eye Color:** blue, black, brown, hazel, green, gray, bloodshot, two different colors
- **Eye Features:** swollen, puffy, crow's feet, wrinkles
- **Facial shapes:**
  - Heart: wider forehead and a narrower chin
  - Square: wide hairline and jawline
  - Pear: small and narrow forehead and larger jawline
  - Round: wide hairline and fullness by the cheekbones
  - Oblong: longer bone structure
  - Oval: longer than wide
  - Diamond: narrow forehead, wide cheeks, narrow chin
- **Facial features:** scars, piercings, tattoos, freckles, wrinkles, moles, acne, smooth, clean-shaven, dimples, dirty, rough, thin, whiskered, youthful, moles, birthmarks, beauty marks, ruddiness (rosacea), blemishes, warts
- **Facial hair:** sideburns, stubble, outgrowth, full or partial beard, goatee, thin, medium, or thick mustache, mustache with handlebars
- **Neck:** slender, thick, muscular, long, medium, short

- **Marks, Scars, Piercings, and Tattoos:** These are excellent identifiers that can rarely be disguised
- **Glasses:** thick, thin, horn-rimmed, clear, or sunglasses

Remember, the more accurate the details you can provide, the better chance law enforcement will have in locating the perpetrator, so develop your powers of observation by practicing describing people you only see for a moment. The day after one of my presentations, a woman called my office and thanked me for the useful advice. She shared that on her way home, she witnessed a robbery on the train platform. Because of my class, she was able to describe the offender perfectly, she said. She wrote down what she observed and gave the information to a police officer who responded to the scene. The officer was amazed by her accurate and detailed description. The offender was caught shortly after with the victim's wallet intact. The police officer said her description helped in catching the thief.

# — CHAPTER 3 —

# ATMs

*"Money often costs too much."*
Ralph Waldo Emerson

CONVENIENCE AND INGENUITY have created a great device that will dispense money without the hassle of going into a bank. Automatic teller machines (ATMs) have come out of necessity in the quick, ever-changing world in which we live. But ATMs are also a gift to thieves because of the likelihood that someone will always be using one to access cash . . . and thieves will always try to take advantage of a situation to take your money or wallet if the opportunity arises.

A thief may also use physical force to get your money. Remember, money can be replaced, but your life cannot. Common sense and good judgment are key to staying safe. According to the Bank Administrative Institute, 40 percent of all ATM crimes occur between 7:00 p.m. and midnight. Always be aware of your surroundings when approaching, using, or leaving an ATM.

## PERSONAL IDENTIFICATION NUMBERS (PINS)

A PIN is the gateway to getting money out of an ATM. Keep this four-digit number secure and confidential at all times. When deciding on a PIN number, avoid common numbers such as birthdays, anniversaries, or your address. Memorize your pin; do not share it with anyone, not even a family member or with anyone over the phone; and *never* write it anywhere on your bank card.

## SAFETY AT AN ATM

When transacting personal monetary business at an ATM, keep a few safety practices in mind. Whenever using an ATM at a bank, store, or other location, if you feel something is "just not right," cancel the transaction immediately, press the clear button, and walk away. If you are using the machine and feel that someone is watching or following you, leave the ATM immediately and go to a familiar, busy area. Call the police, and give them a detailed description of the person(s) and the vehicle and license plates on the car if possible.

Here are some additional safety tips for using ATMs:

- Always have your debit card out and ready to go before approaching the ATM.
- Stand squarely in front of the ATM, and shield the screen and keypad with your body. Always cover the keypad with your free hand when entering your PIN at an ATM, especially if you feel that someone is looking over your shoulder or if someone can see the screen or keypad.
- If someone gets too close to you or tries to engage in conversation with you or tries to help you, tell them politely to step back and that you will be done shortly. If they still advance, cancel the transaction completely and walk away. Never allow a stranger to assist you or offer assistance in any way with your transaction. Be wary if they insist.
- If your card gets jammed in the ATM and it does not come out, do not reenter your PIN. Cancel the transaction, and cancel your card immediately.
- Beware of hidden cameras planted by a thief, which can capture a PIN. Thieves can gather your information and use that to drain your account.
- Watch for card skimmers, which can record your debit card information when using the ATM. Look for the card reader that may be scratched, have tape or glue on it, or may be bulkier than normal or

loose. Skimmers may be difficult to see, and they may be a different color than the ATM.
- Remove your bank card immediately if there is a sticky substance by the card reader or noticeable resistance when putting your bank card into the card reader.
- Be wary if the magnetic strip on your card cannot be read. Notify your bank or credit union, especially if you are sure that your transaction was denied but should have been approved.
- Always take the ATM receipt; never put it in the trash receptacle.
- Always check your ATM transactions against your bank statements to ensure they agree. Contact the bank if there are any discrepancies, unwanted withdrawals, or unauthorized charges made to your account.

Ways to make using an ATM safe include:
- leaving expensive jewelry at home when using an ATM;
- always using a trusted bank's ATM where you feel safe and comfortable, one that has recording surveillance cameras;
- avoiding ATMs that are in malls, sports venues, bars, corners of buildings, low-traffic areas, and dark or desolate areas;
- remembering that someone in the crowded store may be watching for a vulnerable person; and
- having someone accompany you when using an ATM outside of a bank.

## DRIVE-THROUGH ATMS

When visiting a drive-through ATM, it is important to be extra cautious, especially when anyone is "hanging around" the machine. Before driving into the lane, be sure you have a clear and unobstructed view of the area. Is it free of trees or shrubs where someone could hide or not be noticed? Here are some additional tips for staying safe:
- Keep your vehicle's engine running, and keep enough room between the car in front of you in case you have to drive away for whatever reason.
- If someone approaches your vehicle on foot, immediately cancel your transaction and drive away.

## — ATMs —

- Keep passenger windows up and doors locked.
- Turn down the radio so you are not distracted.
- If the lights at the ATM are out or appear not to be working, do not use the machine.
- Almost all ATMs have security cameras posted near them. They also have an additional camera taping the transaction. Many ATM machines at banks and credit unions have monitoring alarm systems.

And remember that according to the US Department of Justice, Office of Community Oriented Policing Services, most ATM crimes involve robbing people of cash after they have made a withdrawal.[5]

---

[5] https://cops.usdoj.gov/RIC/Publications/cops-p017-pub.pdf

# CHAPTER 4

# PICKPOCKETS

*"An investment in knowledge pays the best interest."*
Benjamin Franklin

WHAT A TERRIBLE feeling knowing that your wallet was just taken from you unexpectedly. Pickpocketing is one of the oldest and craftiest professions in the world. These thieves have perfected an art and are like magicians, skilled at using sleight of hand and distractions to take a person's property. They are quick and excellent at what they do, leaving a person vulnerable and defenseless.

Pickpockets rarely get caught because they practice often, and they know just what to say if ever questioned, denying any criminal involvement. They are often very well dressed and soft spoken, and they blend in with the crowd and their environment.

They sometimes work alone or can work with two or three accomplices. A true misconception is that all offenders, especially pickpockets, are male. While a large number of offenders are male, a lot of female offenders also roam the streets looking for an easy target. When pickpockets work in teams, a pretty woman is often used as a distraction, especially when the target is a vulnerable older man. They often flirt and engage in provocative conversation. Older men make the perfect victims because they often have larger amounts of cash on them, will rarely run after the offender, and their memory may not be as keen as it once was.

Pickpockets often use their crafty skills during rush hour. Congestion produces distraction. When teams take a victim's wallet, they pass it quickly to someone on their team before the unsuspecting victim realizes their valuables and wallet are gone. They are always watching to avoid detection and the police. Expert pickpockets use their thumb and forefinger in a swift and delicate manner to commit the crime, rarely ever going deep into someone's pocket. Always be aware if someone gets very close to you or jostles you.

A few distractions used by pickpockets include:
- Asking for directions
- Pretending they know you
- Street performance
- Two people arguing
- To suddenly stop walking in front of you
- Going up an escalator
- Dropping coins
- Falling down in a crowd of people
- Trying to sell something
- Spilling something on a person and then helping to clean it up
- Opening a person's bag by concealing their hands with a newspaper or coat
- Taking advantage of people who are drunk or asleep
- Placing signs warning that pickpockets are in the area so people check to ensure their valuables are in place

## TOURISTS AS TARGETS

Pickpockets are in every city, and no one is immune to becoming a victim, especially when traveling to another city, state, or country. Tourists who visit another country often stand out because of their appearance. They can also be compromised because they may not be familiar with the area, the people, or the foreign currency. Tourists often expect everyone to be honest.

Pickpocket teams often look for travelers who visit popular destinations in the area, including:
- Crowded trains and train platforms
- Crowded and congested buses and where tour buses gather

- Outside hotels and in hotel lobbies
- Tourist attractions and where large crowds often gather
- Crowded stores and parks
- Racetracks and night clubs

The pickpocket's logic is simple: tourists have money in their pockets and are often paying attention only to the scenery, not the crowd.

When traveling, leave expensive jewelry safe and secure at home. And as always, try not to display a lot of money in public, especially when traveling alone. Use common sense when you are visiting from out of town, and try not to look or act like a tourist in the city you are visiting. Wearing a camera around your neck and looking at a map on the street are prominent indications that you are either lost or unfamiliar with the area. The concierge at a larger hotel is often very knowledgeable about where and how to get to your destination in an easy, smart, and safe way.

## CONVENTIONS

Pickpockets know that a majority of conventioneers are from out of town, thus making them perfect targets, especially while they wander outside the convention area. Do not wear any indicators or identifiers outside the convention area where you are attending a conference. These identifiers often include your name and where you are from and can be spotted easily outside the convention. Pickpockets know there is a good chance you are carrying additional money and credit cards.

Conventioneers may attend local liquor establishments and party venues thrown by business clients each evening of the conference. Many conventioneers walk or use local transportation, which could easily make them a target. Being inebriated adds to their vulnerability and puts them in danger of pickpockets succeeding at their craft.

## MAKE YOURSELF PICKPOCKET-PROOF

Whether you are traveling far or just spending a day or evening on your own, there are a few precautions you can take to avoid becoming a victim of a pickpocket. Women should keep their wallets in smaller purses; keeping a wallet in a larger purse makes it easier to take. I recommend that men keep a rubber band over their wallet or money. The friction rubbing against their clothing may alert them of the theft. I also recommend men put their valuables and wallets in their front pockets and keep their hands in their front pockets to prevent anything from being taken. If a gentleman keeps touching his back pocket, an alert pickpocket may catch on that the victim has money.

## OTHER SAFETY TIPS FOR TOURISTS

I recommend photographing your ID (passport, driver's license), airline tickets, and all credit cards and the 800 numbers associated with them. Keep these photocopies separate, and if you are traveling internationally, make sure you have access to the information for the consulate general for your country in case it is needed.

Captain John Doherty of the Chicago Police Department advises,

> While in public, it is critically important to understand the need to walk with confidence and show personal strength. Keep your head up, and recognize potentially bad situations. Law enforcement is thin across the country and limited across the world, which adds a level of insecurity because of your lack of knowledge of an area. When planning a vacation, one added step you can take is to research the areas where you plan to spend time for crime statistics—the types of crime prevalent in the area you will visit and their frequency.

Even if a pickpocket is caught, the likelihood of the victim showing up in court to testify is almost nonexistent. If there is no victim to the crime to serve as a witness, the thief often will not be charged in court and will go free.

## — CHAPTER 5 —

# Identity Theft and Credit Card Fraud

*"If we do not act now to safeguard our privacy,
we could all become victims of identity theft."*
Bill N.

ACCORDING TO THE US Department of Justice (DOJ), "Identity theft and identity fraud are terms used to refer to all types of crime in which someone wrongfully obtains and uses another person's personal data in some way that involves fraud and deception, typically for economic gain."[6]

With enough identifying information about an individual, a criminal can take over someone's identity to conduct a wide range of crimes. For example:
- False applications for loans and credit cards
- Fraudulent withdrawals from bank accounts
- Fraudulent use of telephone calling cards or online accounts
- Obtaining other goods or privileges that the criminal might be denied if he were to use his real name.

Identity theft includes taking another person's name, social security number, or other identifying information, such as their date of birth or their

---

[6] https://www.justice.gov/criminal-fraud/identity-theft/identity-theft-and-identity-fraud

mother's maiden name. It includes a thief using a victim's credit card as their own to defraud retail and online businesses for goods and services. Assuming a person's identity can also affect their credit by fraudulently using a victim's identification to open up bank accounts and secure mortgages and property.

"In the United States, credit card fraud was one of the most common forms of identity theft in four of the last five years. The United States is the country with the most fraud and makes up more than a third of global credit card fraud losses."[7]

You may not realize that you are a victim of identity theft until the theft is well underway. If you do not pay your bills on time, you're not surprised if you are turned down for credit or a loan. But being turned down for a purchase, loan, or mortgage when you have good credit should raise some red flags.

There is nothing like a good story to bring my point across. I was teaching a class on identity theft when a young man named Phil wanted to explain what had happened to him recently. He said that he was embarrassed for being so foolish but wanted to share his story to prevent others from experiencing the same predicament. Phil explained that he used his bank debit card to pay for everything. His paycheck was automatically deposited into his checking account every two weeks.

One day when his bank statement arrived, he looked at the balance as he usually did and noticed a gas purchase for twenty dollars from a gas station in San Diego, California, a city he had never visited. Phil immediately called his bank and asked to have this erroneous charge removed, thinking it was a one-time mistake. The person from his bank explained that there had been many small charges for gas over the course of the year. The total he was out was well over $1,500. Phil was able to get most of his money returned, and he had this valuable piece of advice to share with everyone: Always check your bank and credit card statements to make sure there are no unknown or unauthorized charges.

If your personal information is stolen, and you fear that you may become a victim of credit card fraud—or worse, a victim of identity theft—you should immediately contact one of the major credit bureaus—Equifax, Experian, or TransUnion—and request a fraud alert on your account. A fraud alert is a notice on your credit report that alerts creditors you are or may be a victim of fraud, including identity theft. A fraud alert can make it harder for someone to open unauthorized accounts in your name.

---

[7] https://mint.intuit.com/blog/planning/credit-card-fraud-statistics/

The credit bureau you initially contact will then alert the other two bureaus that credit cards and personal information may have been compromised. Your next step is to file a detailed police report about the credit cards and personal information that was stolen. With a completed police report, a victim of identity theft can go to the Federal Trade Commission (FTC) website at Identitytheft.gov to report a stolen identity and get a personalized recovery plan.

Some of my recommendations for avoiding identity theft include:

- Be careful about revealing your social security, bank account, credit card, and driver's license numbers to just anyone who asks for them.
- Never put a social security number on personal or business checks.
- Use a unique and strong password for each website you access, one that can't be easily duplicated by a hacker.
- Be careful about using your Google or Facebook password to sign into websites. On their website, LifeLock by Norton discusses the downsides to social sign-in you should consider.[8]
- Using two-step authorization and a password manager are the two most important things you can do to protect your online data. Wirecutter.com tested dozens of paid and free sites and concluded the two best are 1Password (paid) and Bitwarden (free).[9]
- Invest in identity theft protection. According to a CNBC website article, "Identity theft protection services monitor websites and databases for signs of your personal information, such as your social security, driver's license number, medical ID and bank account numbers."[10]
- Investigate if you are denied a loan when your credit is very good.
- Put a lock on your mailbox.
- Keep track of all financial assets.
- Monitor credit accounts, pension accounts, bank statements, and investment portfolios.
- Shred any paperwork that identifies you or contains any personal information.
- Destroy extra copies of credit card receipts.

---

[8] https://lifelock.norton.com/learn/identity-theft-resources/is-it-safe-to-sign-in-with-facebook-or-google
[9] https://www.nytimes.com/wirecutter/reviews/best-password-managers/
[10] https://www.cnbc.com/select/what-is-identity-theft-protection/

In a personal interview, Michael Franzese, a former mob boss for the Colombo crime family in New York City, told me, "Today, the biggest crime is identity theft. I believe one out of four people in the United States have reported they were a victim of identity theft. That is an astounding number. I have had my identity stolen and my credit cards compromised. These criminals are targeting individuals like you and me. They have become so sophisticated it is unbelievable. I use a company called IdentityIQ.com, and they monitor everything that I am doing, so I do not have to worry. I do not want to become a victim again."

---

**No One Is Immune to Identity Theft**

Prior to his retirement, a Chicago Police officer experienced the theft of his own identity.

> Several of the officers in my police district and I were victims of identity theft. The stolen information was used to defraud unemployment insurance and gain false payments. I was told by human resources that over two thousand department members were victims, and they suspected it was an inside job from headquarters.
>
> I recommend everyone set up fraud alerts and a freeze at each of the three credit bureaus. The freeze and fraud alerts prevent anyone from opening any accounts with compromised personal information. This is only an inconvenience if you intend to secure a line of credit or loan, which would require removing the freeze temporarily. The alternative is much worse, as I experienced: no assistance from CPD and a reduction of my FICO score as I was left to sort out the mess myself.

---

Your personal information is often compromised when you aren't even aware that you're vulnerable. Let's look at some of the many ways criminals may steal your identity.

## SHOULDER SURFING

When someone gets a little too close physically, they can peek over your shoulder to obtain your personal information. The offender will try to memorize passwords on electronic devices or PIN numbers on credit cards or when you use an ATM machine. Be extremely cautious, and keep a watchful eye on anyone near or behind you, especially when entering personal information into a device at any time.

## GIVING PERSONAL INFORMATION OVER THE PHONE

Many victims are duped into giving out personal information over the phone by an unscrupulous and deceiving offender. Once the offender has your personal information, they can open up bank accounts, credit cards, and mortgages. It is not uncommon for victims to report they were duped into giving their bank account number, social security number, date of birth, or mother's maiden name.

## DUMPSTER DIVING

As a society, we have become accustomed to throwing away junk mail. Thieves rely on our carelessness. A person looking through garbage may not just be looking for cans or food but may be searching for pertinent information they can use to steal a person's identity. Thieves have been known to rummage through trash looking for credit card bills, credit card applications, bank statements, or other items that may contain personal information. The thief will contact the credit card company and request that a new credit card be sent to a different address to divert mail to another location.

## STOLEN CREDIT APPLICATIONS

Even though tampering with the mail is a federal offense, thieves will attempt to steal anything that may contain personal information. This correspondence may include bills, credit cards, credit card applications, or blank checks. But an offer of access to thousands of dollars through a preapproved credit card stolen from a mailbox (or even the trash) is an identity thief's dream.

The thief fills out the credit card application with the victim's name but changes the address, most often to an abandoned building or someplace where they have access to the mail. Once the credit card arrives, the thief purchases something relatively small and actually pays for the item. They may do this for a few months to establish a good history with the credit card company. The thief may even ask for a credit increase and receive a higher credit limit. Finally, the thief will buy an expensive item and not pay for it. After months of trying to collect from the victim at an address where the victim had never lived or worked, the credit card company will mark the victim's account as past due. This will ultimately lower the victim's credit rating.

## SKIMMING

I am amazed by how blatant and sophisticated thieves have become. Thieves have been known to steal credit and debit card information by using a special card reader that copies personal information when using ATM machines and other devices where cards are swiped.

A variation on this involves cashiers double-swiping a credit or debit card when their victim is not paying attention. Here's how it happened to a friend of mine.

Michelle usually gets her morning coffee at the same coffee shop near her house. That particular day, she had a meeting downtown and went to the same shop's downtown location. As Michelle was ordering, she noticed the person behind the counter put her card through two different machines. After questioning the employee and being unsatisfied with her answer, Michelle called the police, who viewed the coffee shop's video footage. After interviewing the employee, the police got her to admit to scanning the information for a major theft ring. The employee said she received ten dollars for every card she could scan into a second card reader. The employee was arrested, and a major theft ring was taken down because Michelle paid attention and then took the appropriate action by getting the police involved.

## CREDIT CARD FRAUD

Credit card fraud is the unauthorized use of a credit or debit card or similar payment tool, such as an automated clearing house (ACH), electronic funds transfer (EFT), or a recurring charge to fraudulently obtain money or property. Credit and debit card numbers can be stolen from unsecured websites or can be obtained in an identity theft scheme. Credit card fraud can happen as a result of stolen, misplaced, or counterfeit credit cards, and the increase in online retail shopping has made credit card fraud (the use of a person's credit card number in e-commerce transactions) more prevalent.

## TIPS TO AVOID CREDIT CARD FRAUD

- Credit card fraud can happen as a result of stolen, misplaced, or counterfeit credit cards.
- Limit the number of credit cards in your wallet.
- Take only the credit card for the store you plan to visit or one major credit card.
- Always make sure you are purchasing from a reputable company or source. Check out the company on Google or Yelp, and be extra cautious when dealing with an individual or company outside of the United States. Unscrupulous individuals will make it extremely difficult for a victim to get their merchandise or money refunded.
- Keep a watchful eye on any cashier handling your credit card. Make sure the clerk does not swipe the card into the card reader or scanner more than once.
- If possible, purchase items online using a major credit card that will stand behind any items purchased. You can often dispute the charges if something goes wrong.

── CHAPTER 6 ──

# Scams

*"Trust your gut. Your gut feelings are usually accurate and correct.
If you truly feel there is something wrong, chances are there is."*
Unknown

PEOPLE WHO WANT to take your money by offering bogus services and must-have products will use the art of deception and greed to convince you to believe what they are saying. American showman P. T. Barnum is remembered for his famous phrase, "There is a sucker born every minute." Michael Franzese, a former mob boss for the Colombo crime family in New York City, told me personally, "Criminals are very smart. If they figure out a way to scam someone, trust me, they will do it."

Criminals try to instill trust and confidence in their victims, otherwise known as "marks." Victims are scammed every day, often through the use of a sad story that plays on the victim's sympathies.

Con artists often target older citizens for a few reasons. An older person's vision and memory may not be razor sharp; they often have money readily available, are less likely to admit they made a mistake that may display incompetence on their part, or are embarrassed for being foolish and do not report the crime.

Common scams include asking for a money transfer by gift card or other means; putting up money to receive a larger sum of money later; and being persuaded or tricked into giving personal information, credit card, or bank information. But there are other scams, some of which are quite sophisticated, and you should always be aware of both the tried-and-true scams and the newer versions that always seem to be popping up. When in doubt, check with someone you trust before deciding to send or give money to someone you don't know.

### A Story Too Good to Be True . . . and It Was

This story is an example of something too good to be true that could have ended badly if I had not trusted my gut feeling. I saw an online ad recently for a 1959 Cadillac Biarritz convertible with less than ten thousand miles on it for about $39,000. This car is easily worth about five times more than that. My first thought was, *Something is wrong. Does this guy realize the price is incredibly low?* My curiosity got the best of me. I sent an email to the person and inquired about this classic vehicle. The gentleman quickly sent me a dozen pictures of the car and a description of all its great features.

I anticipated exactly what happened next. He gave his name and explained that he was working in the oil industry on a tanker in the Gulf of Mexico and was not available to deal with me personally in the sale of the car. He said the car was with a broker in Seattle, Washington, and they had his permission to handle the transaction and all the paperwork involved. He would like the deal to go quickly. He indicated that I must send a wire transfer of $20,000 to hold and secure the convertible so no one else could buy it. As a former cop, I was suspicious. I Googled his name; I learned that he did work in the oil industry, but that was all I could find. Next, I emailed him for the auto broker's name and address in Seattle and told him I was retired and wanted to see and drive the car and would gladly travel to Seattle. I sent a second email telling him that I wanted to visibly see and hold the actual vehicle title when I went to see the car. I made it clear that I would not consider the deal otherwise. He made one more futile attempt to have me wire the money. Needless to say, I never heard from him again.

> My point: if someone else had been lured into this bogus interaction, they would have surely lost $20,000 by wire-transferring their hard-earned money and would never have received the Cadillac.
>
> Remember the old saying: if it is too good to be true, it probably is!

## CHAIN LETTERS

I remember my parents receiving a few chain letters in the mail, asking them to send fifty dollars to the person at the top of the list, with the promise that following the instructions to put their name and address at the bottom of the list and mail that list to ten of their friends would net them hundreds of dollars. Fifty dollars was a lot of money back then, and many people could be enticed by the thought of receiving a windfall. My dad was smart enough to know this was a scam and told my mom, sister, and me never to fall for something like that. I remember my dad ripping up the bogus request and throwing it into the trash.

According to the United States Postal Inspection Service, "A chain letter is a 'get rich quick' scheme that promises that your mailbox will soon be stuffed full of cash if you decide to participate. You're told you can make thousands of dollars every month if you follow the detailed instructions in the letter."[11]

Chain letters are illegal if sent through the United States Postal Service. That should tell you a lot.

## CHARITABLE DONATIONS

Many people use charitable donations to help others in need, while others use them as a tax write-off. No matter why you decide to give to your favorite charity, ensure that your hard-earned money is going to a legitimate 501(c)(3) tax-exempt charity organization. According to Foundation Group, the terms *nonprofit*, *501(c)(3)*, and *tax-exempt* do not all mean the same thing.

---

[11] https://www.fightfraudamerica.com/wire/mail/chain_letters.html

> Nonprofit means the entity, usually a corporation, is organized for a nonprofit purpose. A nonprofit organization that has been recognized by the [Internal Revenue Service] IRS as being tax-exempt by virtue of its charitable programs is a 501(c)(3). Tax-exemption is the result of a nonprofit organization being recognized by the IRS as being organized for any purpose allowable under 501(c)(3)–501(c)(27).[12]

Just because the material is presented to you in a brochure does not necessarily mean it is true. Do your due diligence, and ensure the charity is legitimate. You should know what percentage is used for administrative costs and who is actually benefiting from your donation.

According to the National Philanthropic Trust, "Americans gave $484.85 billion in 2021. This reflects a 4% increase from 2020."[13] To avoid charity scams, the Federal Trade Commission (FTC) suggests, "When you decide to support a cause you care about, you want your donation to count. Doing some research and planning your giving can help ensure your donations get where they will do good."[14]

Be very cautious of paid solicitors who work on behalf of a so-called fraternal organization or charity. Many people have been duped into thinking they are helping their local law enforcement or firefighters by sending money to organizations representing them. All police, firefighters, and other first responders are paid through taxes received from their prospective towns or cities. Con artists saying they represent the Fraternal Order of Police or a firefighters' union may give pennies on the dollar to an organization, but in reality, it is truly a fraud. They are very convincing and will go out of their way to get your money, even coming by your home to pick up a check. If you really want to show your appreciation to any first responder, just thank them for their service—trust me, they will appreciate that very much.

Some deceptive charities manage their operations outside of the United States and operate outside of the law. Legitimate charities gladly accept checks

---

[12] https://www.501c3.org/frequently-asked-questions/does-nonprofit-501c3-and-tax-exempt-all-mean-the-same-thing/
[13] https://www.nptrust.org/philanthropic-resources/charitable-giving-statistics/
[14] https://consumer.ftc.gov/features/how-donate-wisely-and-avoid-charity-scams

or credit card payments. If a donation to a charity is sent by check or major credit card and the charity is not legitimate, a dispute with the bank or credit card company could be possible if you act within a certain amount of time.

Be leery of anyone insisting on cash, gift cards, or a wire transfer because these are obviously scams. The charity you think you are helping will never get the money, and you will never recover your money.

Here are my recommendations:
- Only give to charities you know and trust as genuine.
- Be suspicious of charities that request cash or gift cards.
- Make checks out to the charitable organization only, never to an individual.
- Never give out any personal information over the phone, even if a charitable organization requests it. This includes your address, date of birth, social security number, or credit card information.
- Be especially cautious if someone from a charity that seems legitimate wants an immediate donation over the phone or by credit card. A legitimate charity is grateful for any donation and will not intimidate you into giving money immediately. Never feel pressured to give money to anyone immediately; it is often a clear indication that you're dealing with a scammer.
- Always ask to see official identification from the organization if you are uncertain about the charity's authenticity.

## CHECK FORGERY

Hundreds of millions of US government checks are issued each year, according to the US Department of the Treasury. This large number, which includes monthly social security payments and income tax refunds, attracts criminals who specialize in stealing and forging them. A high percentage of the thefts are from mailboxes in apartment complexes and private homes, and losses from check thefts and forgeries amount to millions of dollars yearly. A check thief usually forges a signature and presents false identification. Retail merchants often unknowingly aid the forger by failing to request proper identification. The merchants suffer the loss when they cash forged checks.

## CRYPTOCURRENCY

Cryptocurrency can be described as a form of digital money. It is just like currency but without paper. It works just like the dollar or euro. It can be compared to assets like stocks and bonds and real estate. Cybercurrency can be accepted in a trade transaction or bartered for any type of goods or services that are completely digital.

These digital currencies are not regulated or maintained by a central monetary authority. Instead, a decentralized system of cryptography is used and commonly accessed through a vast computer network.[15]

Bitcoin is one kind of cryptocurrency and is widely recognized as the most popular one to date; others are called *altcoins*. Bitcoin's rise has allowed the general public to get acquainted with cryptocurrencies as it has started to break into the mainstream, allowing criminals a new avenue to gain their victims' trust. The scams themselves often resemble those discussed in this book, with the difference being the use of digital currencies. Forbes.com reports that "Crypto scams are like any other financial scam, except the scammers are after your crypto assets rather than your cash."[16] Once these innocent victims relinquish their money, it will rarely be recovered.

Many recent scams have involved cryptocurrency. According to the FTC, cryptocurrency scammers have stolen more than $1 billion since 2021.[17]

## EXTENDED WARRANTIES

Be cautious if you receive a phone call or email indicating that your warranty on an appliance or vehicle is about to expire and the item in question will be without coverage for a costly repair or expense. You will be told to register on a website that asks for personal information, such as your bank account or credit card, log-in ID, and password. Do your due diligence, and inquire directly to the company, store, or dealer that originally initiated the deal.

---

[15] https://dailyillini.com/sponsored/2022/10/18/what-are-cryptocurrencies/
[16] https://www.forbes.com/advisor/investing/cryptocurrency/top-crypto-scams/
[17] https://www.techtarget.com/whatis/feature/Common-cryptocurrency-scams

## FAKE WEBSITES

The internet has brought a myriad of phony websites that appear authentic for a legitimate business or company. The uniform research locator (URL) is the browser's internet address, resource, or identifier. Closely examine the URL at the top of the address bar on the computer screen to determine whether the website is legitimate. Many phony websites contain misspelled words or all numbers at the beginning of the URL.

A legitimate website has a security system in place, indicated by "HTTPS://" at the beginning of the URL. "HTTPS transmits its data security using an encrypted connection. Basically, it uses a public key which is then decrypted on the recipient side. The public key is deployed on the server and included in what you know as an SSL certificate."[18] Many websites will show a little icon of a padlock in the upper left-hand corner of the URL, which often indicates a higher level of security. In my safety classes, I assured everyone that this small padlock assures you that the site is safe; just remember that there is never a 100 percent guarantee that any site is secure. It is important to research who is asking for any information by checking the search engine.

Scams sometimes occur when someone is searching for information and looking for support; an example is using Google to locate Amazon support. Scammers set up a phony support link that looks like a genuine Amazon support site. The victim is instructed to give personal information or is redirected to another link "to address the problem"—but the scammer controls the site. There, the scammer indicates a refund is due or suggests other bogus money issues can be resolved. The scammers ask for personal and bank information that will give them the ability to withdraw money from your bank account, often until the money is depleted. Be wary of any website that asks you to reenter or reaffirm your personal information when you've given it previously.

If you use online shopping or pay bills through the internet, it is imperative to use a secure website. Never give out any credit card information unless you are highly confident that the site is secure and trustworthy. And I recommend using firewalls, antispyware, or antivirus software to help protect the valuable and personal information stored in your computer.

---

[18] https://www.keycdn.com/blog/difference-between-http-and-https

## FORTUNE-TELLING

People who are desperate may turn to fortune-tellers for answers that will help them with love, relationships, and financial and other problematic issues in their lives. This scam has been around for decades, and thousands of people have been duped out of millions of dollars.

The Romani culture is known for *divination* or fortune-telling, which is always practiced by women. Through careful listening and the art of persuasion, they learn enough intimate details about what is wrong or is bothering their victim to tell that person what they want to hear. The fortune-teller soon tries to find out how much money their victim has readily available. She will associate the victim's bad luck with a curse and convince that person that she has a solution to their misfortune. She persuades the trusting and anxious victim that she can remove the curse, starting by blessing their money. At some point in the ceremony, the real money the victim has given over is switched for a bag of shredded paper, which is then burned to lift the curse, leaving the victim's real money in the hands of the fortune-teller. The ritual of the fortune-teller switching the money in a paper bag often occurs at a discrete and remote location. Not all fortune-teller scams happen this way, but the idea is the same; they always involve bait and switch.

## HOME REPAIR

One of the most common types of complaints and problems with contractors or handymen is home repair scams. While there are hundreds of legitimate contractors who do a good job, there are a few that prey on individuals through phony or false advertising.

Nick Sposato, the alderman of the 38th Ward in Chicago, has the following advice.

> Home repair is a common scam. The work is often poorly done if it is even done at all. Some of these con artists start the job and never come back to finish. When questioned, they say they will

be back to finish "in an hour or a little later," and that's the last the homeowner sees of them.

Paying a deposit for materials isn't unusual, but in a common scam, the delivered material may be of poor quality, or it may not be delivered at all.

Homeowners are often exploited by individuals trying to sell additional construction material that was "left over from a job down the street." When questioned, they say they will be back to finish "in an hour or a little later."

It is important to only hire someone to fix up your house from referrals or other trusted sources. My advice: do not deal with strangers knocking on your door.

## IMPERSONATING A POLICE OFFICER

Henry Perez, an officer with the Senior Services Unit of the Chicago Police, told me about a police impersonation scam in his district. A senior citizen was followed out of a bank, and he heard a knock at his door soon after arriving home. Two men posing as police officers told the senior citizen that they were investigating a teller at his bank who was exchanging fake money for real money. The police impersonators asked to see the money he had just withdrawn. After examining the money, one of the offenders exclaimed, "Yes, these are fake. We need to inventory this for evidence." They immediately put the money in an envelope and gave the senior a receipt for the money taken, and then instructed him to go to the bank the next day and collect the real money.

As instructed, the senior victim took the receipt to the bank to collect his "real" money. He soon learned he had been scammed out of $800.

## INVESTMENTS

Investment scam artists present their bogus "investment opportunity" as a "once in a lifetime deal, and if you do not act immediately, your chances of making money will dwindle significantly." These con artists incorporate high-pressure tactics and learn to circumvent any rejection or refusal they encounter. They promote the investment's high yield with little or no risk as a fantastic opportunity. It is not uncommon for these con artists to impersonate someone from an investment firm using phony but realistic-looking websites to encourage a victim to act immediately because "If you snooze, you'll lose." Once the duped individual sends their money (usually via a wire transfer or other money transfer source), they rarely ever recover any of their funds.

Other investment scams include offers that involve real estate, such as worthless land or property that has little or no value. Their sales pitch includes overwhelming pressure to act immediately, that their offer is only good for that day, or that the deal will not last. Stress and tension lead to poor rational thinking and hasty decisions. Getting something for nothing means the criminal gets your money, and you get nothing. If it sounds too good to be true, it probably is.

## IRS

Everyone worries about getting a notice from the IRS because they made a mistake on their tax return. Scammers prey on this fear by calling taxpayers and saying they are the IRS, and their end goal is to scare innocent victims into sending money or gift cards to them.

Remember these two things: first, the IRS will only send correspondence via the United States Post Office; and second, the IRS will never call on the phone. Many people do not realize this and panic when they pick up the phone and are told the person calling is from the IRS. The criminal is often calling from India or another foreign country and does not speak the English language very well. The scammer will give their victim an agent ID number, and when questioned, they deflect. They use scare tactics to convince the victim that federal agents will come to their home or place of business to arrest them for not paying the money they supposedly owe.

Remember this: *The IRS will never call you on the phone for any money owed.* And as I've urged before, never agree to send money, give credit card information, or give any bank account information to someone who contacts you over the phone.

## LOTTERY

Many people play the lottery with hopes and dreams of winning enormous wealth. A scammer will either email or call someone claiming it is their "lucky" day and telling them they won a lot of money in the lottery. The only problem is that they never bought a lottery ticket, or they cannot remember, thinking they might have. The scammer tells the intended victim that they need to consent to terms by sending money for taxes, fees, and other conditions to receive their money so they can claim the exorbitant cash prize. The victim soon finds out that their lottery check is not worth the paper it is printed on.

Another ploy used by scammers is the promise of a direct deposit of lottery winnings. The supposed lottery winner is instructed to open the link on a specific website so money can be deposited directly into their account. This link takes the victim to an information page that requests personal information, bank account information, log-in information, and passwords. The victim, thinking they will receive a windfall of money, soon finds out their bank account has been drained.

## OVERPAYMENT

Numerous people sell items they no longer need. There are many sites that offer a service to match sellers with potential buyers. Scammers trick the unsuspecting seller by saying they are very interested in the item for sale but are out of town or personally unavailable to get the merchandise. They will pay the asking price by check, money order, or bank check, but they tell the seller they will send an extra $100 and then ask the seller to do them a favor: give the extra cash to the person who is going to pick up the item so they can get paid.

The seller will often receive the bogus check on Saturday afternoon when most banks are closed. The seller will have to wait to deposit the check when the bank opens on Monday. The scammer arranges for an accomplice to pick up the merchandise on Saturday. Thinking the check is legitimate, the seller graciously gives the $100 and the merchandise to the courier. When the seller deposits the check, they'll learn it is fake or fraudulent. The seller not only gave their item away but spent money to do so.

Not all scams use these dollar amounts, but they are all similar in nature. The scammers will always send extra money and have someone else pick up the item. In my experience, this is a common scam on Craigslist, but it is not exclusive to that site.

## PACKAGE DELIVERY

Tens of thousands of people purchase millions of items over the internet every day, and this has made package delivery a favorite target of many scammers. The criminal will send out a bogus email or text from FedEx, UPS, DHL, or the United States Postal Service (USPS) that a package in their name is waiting to be shipped with a tracking link, often with a notice about an unexpected delay that must be addressed. When the victim clicks on the link, the best-case result is additional annoying emails leading to potential fraud; the worst-case result is identity theft or loss of funds, or both.

The Federal Trade Commission advises, "National delivery companies are also providing information on their websites to help consumers avoid falling for package delivery scams." They share a link to the US Postal Inspection Service's alert about phony delivery texts, which cites "unsolicited mobile text messages indicating that a USPS delivery is awaiting your action and includes a non-postal service web link to click."[19]

## PAYPAL

Another online scam involves spoofing PayPal. You receive an email announcing "action required regarding your PayPal account." The carefully worded email suggests your PayPal account has been compromised or restricted due to fraudulent activity, and you must call the number in the email to have your account amended and unlocked. When you call the number, you are asked to verify your identity before action can be taken. The scammer will use the personal and bank account information you give them to drain your bank accounts.

---

[19] https://www.fcc.gov/how-identify-and-avoid-package-delivery-scams

## PHISHING

No matter how official or legitimate an email may appear, be leery of any asking you to update or verify personal information. As we have established, this information might be used to obtain a loan or mortgage, open a bank account, obtain credit cards, acquire goods and services, or shop using online accounts. Pay close attention to the web browser address, and look for subtle changes in letters and numbers. The letter O could be replaced with a zero, or the lowercase l could be replaced with the number 1.

According to Experian,

> Phishing is an attempt to get recipients to divulge sensitive information such as usernames, passwords or social security numbers, or to transfer money to the scammer through a variety of methods. Usually, this is done through email, but phishing via text message is becoming more common. . . . It is worth keeping an eye out for these scams year-round, but you may see certain scams pick up around certain times of the year. For example, phishing for tax information is common at the beginning of the year, and phishing targeted at shoppers ramps up around the holidays when a lot of people are buying gifts.[20]

Many people are blindsided when they realize their personal identity has been stolen. In addition to being denied a loan for which you should qualify, other indications are being billed for an item you did not receive or an ATM transaction you did not authorize. You may also learn that a credit card was issued in your name that has been used but you never applied for, or that your mail has been redirected to another location.

## PIGEON DROP

This scam is one of the oldest around, but it is still popular. Two con artists approach someone they hope is naïve near a bus stop or a busy store or in a

---

[20] https://www.experian.com/blogs/ask-experian/how-to-avoid-phishing-scams/

mall parking lot. They tell their victim that they found an envelope full of cash and open it to reveal what appears to be a lot of money (but is often just a few $100 bills in the front followed by a stack of singles behind). Both scammers ask the intended victim what they should do with the money, saying they will split it three ways with their intended victim.

One of the con artists may suggest that the money came from illegal activity (possibly drugs or gambling), so they should not get the police involved. The other con artist will say they work for a lawyer who will know what to do with it. The presumed lawyer is called, and he suggests they each put up "good faith money" because it may take some time to divvy up the money if no one claims it. Each con artist puts $2,000 in the envelope, but for that amount of money, the victim may have to go to the bank to withdraw their share of the earnest money. After the victim puts their money into the envelope, the con artist switches that envelope with one of similar weight, but it isn't until the con artists leave that the victim is left holding a worthless envelope full of paper.

"My experience with the Pigeon Drop scam was personal," Chicago Police Senior Service Officer Henry Perez told me. "My own mother was a victim of this scam."

> Mom was waiting for the bus by the University of Illinois Hospital, where she worked as a custodian. She was approached by two women carrying a shopping bag. They told my mother they had something for her. They opened up the shopping bag, and it looked like a bag full of money. They told my mother that they would split all of that money with her if she put some of her money into the shopping bag. My mom said she only had twenty dollars, so they boldly offered to take her to her bank. My mom agreed and entered their car, parked nearby. They drove her to her credit union, where she withdrew twelve hundred dollars. She got back in the car and gave them the money to put in the bag. They asked my mom if she had any more money, and she said, "No, but I have some jewelry at the house." When they drove my mother to her house, my father was home, and he asked my mom what

she was doing and who those strangers in the car were. My mom lied and said, "Friends from work." My mom ended up taking a handful of gold jewelry and putting all of it in their bag. She reentered the car, and then they drove her back to work. There, they gave her the shopping bag and told her a doctor from her hospital would soon be by to split the money. She waited for a long time after the women left. Finally, she opened the bag to find about thirty dollars in loose singles, and the rest was just paper. My mom started crying.

## PONZI SCHEMES

A Ponzi scheme is an investment fraud in which participants are promised high returns with little to no risk on their investments, but the older investors are paid with funds put in by later investors. These profitable speculations are often purported to be in stocks and volatile investments, but often there is no legitimate business involved.

The Ponzi scheme was named in the 1920s after Charles Ponzi, who reaped thousands of dollars for himself as many people went bankrupt because of his ruse. A well-known modern Ponzi scheme, one of the largest in modern history, was run by Bernie Madoff, who swindled thousands of investors out of millions of dollars.

When seeking out a reputable broker, financial advisor, brokerage, or investment firm, it is important to do your due diligence. An investor can contact the Financial Industry Regulatory Authority (FINRA), which operates as a self-regulatory organization under the federal government's Securities and Exchange Commission. Not only is it imperative to research the investment firm thoroughly but also to understand the investment and its risks. Be skeptical of a high-percentage return in a short time, unregistered investments from an unlicensed broker, or a broker with negative reviews; these can often be signs to not invest. As I said before, if something is too good to be true, it probably is.

## POST-DISASTER RELIEF

Scammers take advantage of people who need help recovering after a natural disaster.

AARP's Fraud Resource Center warns that not only do dubious contractors descend on affected communities, but some who claim to work for the Federal Emergency Management Agency (FEMA) prey on struggling homeowners by promising help in the form of grants, building permits, or help speeding up insurance claims—for a deposit or fee.

Scammers may also pretend to be representatives of the relief effort and ask for personal information. Not only are the victims devasted because of the disaster they have encountered, but there is a good chance they will become victims of identity theft. My suggestion is to contact FEMA directly. Remember, there is never a fee to receive money from FEMA for any disaster.

A genuine FEMA inspector will not ask for money or personal information.[21] If you are worried about contractors who call or come to you door, especially after a disaster, ask for referrals from previous customers and if possible, inspect their previous work. Confirming their business with your local Better Business Bureau for any complaints is highly recommended.

## PUBLIC PHONE CHARGERS

With new technology comes a greater possibility of fraud. This is especially true when thieves take only minutes to hack into public phone chargers. This deceptive practice is called *juice jacking*. An unsuspecting and trusting victim notices a public cell phone charging station and without hesitation uses it to charge their phone. What the person does not realize is that a hacker secretly installed malware into this device. This malware gives the thief full access to all the information on that person's phone without having to be in the vicinity. The hacker will have access to all previous phone calls, text messages, contacts, phone numbers, bank account information, passwords, and even photos. It only takes one time for a person's phone to be infected and the thief will have access to the victim's phone forever.

---

[21] https://www.aarp.org/money/scams-fraud/info-2019/disaster.html

An easy way to avoid this scam is to always carry a portable phone charger. These chargers reliably provide additional power when needed and are well worth the investment.

## PYRAMID SCHEMES

Pyramid schemes have been around for decades. An initial promoter seeks out investors to buy into a fraudulent investment. Each investor, in turn, will need to recruit two other people to invest in the scheme, paying the person at the top of the pyramid in order for them to join and participate.

The pyramid scheme only benefits the few people who start it or invest in it early. Pyramid schemes can involve products as well. This ploy is called a pyramid because, at each level, the number of participants increases. Mathematically, if the pyramid continues to grow, there will not be enough people in the world to sustain it.

There are many different names associated with pyramid schemes, such as *gifting circles* or *sharing circles*. My dad was approached a few times to participate in a pyramid investment. He declined, but my uncle invested $500, which he never recovered. My dad warned him, but my uncle wouldn't listen.

The best way to avoid pyramid schemes is to do your homework and not invest quickly. Remember, it's *your* money at risk. Try to gather as much information as possible about the company or product involved. Who are the principal officers or promoters of the company? Do you have to involve other friends or relatives to move up and secure your initial investment? Are you obligated to purchase the product or the service or to become a distributor? Read the fine print, or have your lawyer read the contract. Speak with others who may have invested, and get their take on the investment. Be especially leery if the startup cost is substantial.

## QR CODES

A QR code is basically an updated version of a bar code; it is a machine-readable optical label that contains information about the specific item it is attached to. The square, black-and-white design can be instantly read by a cell phone's camera. QR codes can be used to view a restaurant's menu, a shop's inventory, or sales at a business. My suggestion is to be cautious using QR codes because they are not all as safe as most younger people tend to believe.

One way crooks deceive their innocent victims is by blatantly placing their own fraudulent QR code stickers over a legitimate business's QR codes.

According to CNET, "Scammers are creating their own malicious QR codes designed to dupe unwitting consumers into handing over their banking or personal information. . . .That's especially true with tech like QR codes, which people know how to use but might not know how they work." Angel Grant, vice president of security at F5, an app security company, says, "It's easier to manipulate people if they don't understand it."

"Scanning the bogus QR codes will not do anything to your phone, such as download malware in the background," CNET advises. "But it will take you to a bogus website designed to get your bank account, credit card, or other personal information."[22] The innocent victim, thinking that the QR code is going to a business website, can actually make a disastrous mistake.

One way to avoid becoming a victim of this crime is to use your fingernail to see if a sticker has been placed over another legitimate QR code. Another way is to use a secure app from your phone's Android or Apple app store that has the capability to screen potential malicious and dishonest sites initiated by QR codes. An example of an app that screens QR codes is Sophos Interceptor. Always be cautious of where a QR code takes you, especially if it is not the intended business or website information or website that you are seeking. Close out the inquiry immediately.

If, for some reason, the QR code being displayed takes you to a different website than what you wanted or expected, I recommend that you immediately close out the link on your phone. Then, call one of the three major credit bureaus and alert them that fraudulent activity may have taken place. Give as much information and as many details as you possibly can. I also recommend contacting the FBI's IC3.gov, which will look into any issues regarding fraudulent internet activity. Next, make a police report, but understand that the police may not be able to help immediately. And my final advice is never to pay a bill using a QR code.

---

[22] https://www.cnet.com/tech/services-and-software/qr-code-scams-are-on-the-rise-heres-how-to-avoid-getting-duped/

## RANSOM FROM GRANDPARENTS

This scam targets senior citizens who are most often living alone. A young person posing as their grandson or granddaughter calls, often late at night or early in the morning, and says they are in serious trouble and need cash right away. The young con artist convinces their "grandparent" that they are the only person the "grandchild" could turn to who could help them, often adding that their parents would be angry if they found out. The grandparent, still half asleep, disorientated, and not thinking clearly, gives them their credit card information. A bold con artist may also send someone to pick up cash from their home.

## ROBOCALLS

Americans are overwhelmed daily with robocalls (computer-generated calls) that try to convince them to take action or buy something. And every day, millions of robocalls are initiated with the intent to defraud people by getting them to put their money into a deceitful investment venture, contest, sweepstakes, or charity.

Another common robocall scam is calling for verification of a large purchase. Scammers hope to get a victim to believe the aggressive voice on the other end of the line about an unrecognized purchase on their account for a large dollar amount, instructing them to "Press one or stay on the line to cancel this purchase." The intended victim, who did not authorize an expensive charge, follows the instructions given, and the typical scam begins with the caller asking for personal information to cancel the fake charge. The scammers now have the victim's personal information and can use it to drain bank accounts or charge items on the victim's credit card.

My recommendation is not to acknowledge or listen to instructions given from a computer-generated call, which may prompt and initiate additional robocalls. Hang up immediately, and block the number on your phone. If you believe your subscription needs to be renewed or your car's warranty has expired, call the company's number on their official website, and speak to a representative. You initiate the call.

A common scammer tactic is saying the caller is with Amazon support, Google support, or Best Buy's Geek Squad. They often sound official as they explain that the victim's subscription for service has expired, and that they need to take care of this problem immediately. The scammers begin to clarify what must be done on the victim's computer. By following the scammer's directions, the unsuspecting person usually gives up control of their computer. From there, it does not take long for the scammers to get passwords and enter their victim's bank accounts or gain personal information for swindling them further. These scammers often work from remote locations across the world, with many traced back to cities in India.

## ROMANCE

People looking for love and companionship is nothing new . . . but the internet has allowed more unscrupulous individuals to use the cloak of love and affection to take advantage of unsuspecting women and men. Whether a victim's loneliness results from a breakup of a long relationship, the death of a spouse or partner, or low self-esteem, someone who is lonesome and looking for companionship, love, or marriage may be duped into believing that someone sincerely cares for them.

These con artists will do whatever they can to start a loving and trusting relationship. They often prey on their isolated victim's loneliness. The con artist is the victim's Prince Charming or their dream come true, someone who takes an interest in them and offers them the happiness they have dreamed about. They become completely overwhelmed by emotion, excitement, and passion. (These personal relationships can be platonic, but they often have the same end result.)

The term "love is blind" is often associated with these scenarios because victims do not see through the ruse. A crafty con artist will play on the forlorn victim's feelings and good-heartedness. The con artist declares feelings of attraction, even if the parties have never met. The attention from the con artist can be awe-inspiring as the victim begins to truly believe they have found that perfect person to spend the rest of their lives with.

The con artist demonstrates trust and confidence as they convince their victim that their love and affection are genuine. The unsuspecting victim believes the impostor's lies and deception. It does not take long for the con artist to "begrudgingly" ask for money, often for some unseen emergency, that they do not have "at the present time." The emergency could be the loss of a job or a death in the family, something significant. They staunchly promise that the money will be paid back quickly. The con artist confirms that this ordeal is just a bump in the road. Some individuals catch on quickly, but others who believe in the con artist may not stop giving until they are out of money and it is too late. After a while, the con artist disappears.

### A Story of a Romantic Con Artist

My wife's friend Betty and her husband moved to Florida. She invited us to stay at their new home for a few days once they were settled. While we were there, I noticed a home for sale right across the street from my wife's friend's home. I went to look at the house and loved it for when I would retire from the police department in a few years. I figured I would rent it out until then to help pay for the mortgage. Betty recommended Michael K. to rent the house. Because she recommended Michael, I did not do my due diligence and check out his credentials and past history. Shame on me.

Well, Betty was quite heavyset and had very low self-esteem. She met a man named Michael on the internet, and he dazzled her with his deceptive charm and adoration. Betty admitted to my wife that she was having an affair with Michael, who treated her like a queen. It was only after a date or two that he "left his wallet at home" or "didn't get his check cashed," and many other bogus reasons why he didn't have money. Betty started paying for everything. The signs were always there, but because he paid attention to her, she ignored them.

What Betty didn't tell us was that this was the same Michael she recommended to rent from us. My wife had told me to check his credit, but because Betty recommended him, I foolishly did not listen nor do my due diligence to protect us. Needless to say, Michael K. conned us from

> day one, never paying any rent and giving us excuse after excuse until we finally had him evicted. We found out that Michael K. had an extensive history of scamming many women out of money, lying, and duping more than twenty female victims. He has never been caught and still thrives on deceit and dishonesty.

## SPOOFING

"Spoofing copies and exploits the identity of your contacts, the look of well-known brands, or the addresses of trusted websites," warns Avast, an antivirus software company. Spoofers pretend to be someone you trust to access sensitive personal information. Three of the most common spoofing attack types are:

- **Email spoofing:** Forged email addresses that are recognizable to the victim seek personal or inside information. Your email's spam filter can be trained to recognize these generic email domains, generic greetings, strange attachments, inconsistencies, and mistakes, forced urgency, and "typo squatting," which takes advantage of common typos people make when entering web addresses.
- **Website spoofing:** Spoofed websites are commonly linked with spoofed emails. They usually look very much like the legitimate site they want you to think you're visiting, and they sometimes use a cloaked URL to direct you through their own system and collect your personal information.
- **Caller ID spoofing:** Robocallers use this type of spoof because they can make their calls appear to come from a specific geographic location or a trusted number.[23]

Other even more sophisticated spoofing methods exist and can be more technically complex, but all "usually involve an element of social engineering,

---

[23] Spoofing information based on Avast.com's webpage, "What Is Spoofing and How Can You Prevent It?" https://www.avast.com/c-spoofing

where scammers psychologically manipulate their victims by playing on human vulnerabilities such as fear, greed, or lack of technical knowledge."[24]

I've mentioned a few scams where the perpetrator uses information about the victim that seems legitimate. I personally became a victim of an email hacker recently, and the fallout has caused no end to inconvenience for me, my family, and my friends.

## I GOT HACKED

Anyone's privacy can be compromised; my own email was hacked.

I must have inadvertently opened up a phishing email. Of course it was accidental, but it still happened.

In addition to writing and speaking, I also oversee my former high school's security team. I get paid by direct deposit on the first and the fifteenth of every month. Recently, the office financial manager called me and asked if I could stop by her office; she said it was urgent, and she needed to speak with me.

Kathy quickly gave me the bad news: she said, "I believe your email has been hacked. Someone is pretending to be you, and they are also trying to get me to send your paycheck to their account under the guise of paying better interest."

Kathy printed out the hacker's emails.

**Friday, March 31, 2023 at 2:48 p.m. (supposedly from me*)**

> Hi, can I get my pay to my account directly? I changed my bank to another offering me a better savings interest last week and was recommended to inform you to update my payroll details. I believe I only need my new account and routing number if I am correct? Also, can it be effective for the next payday? Please get back to me as soon as possible. (*Note:

---

[24] https://www.kaspersky.com/resource-center/definitions/spoofing

This person used additional personal information about me in the signature line to convince my employer that these emails were from me.)

**Friday, March 31, 2023 at 4:35 p.m.**

Hello, did you get my last email?

**Friday, March 31, 2023 at 9:49 p.m.**

Kathy wrote back:

> Ron, can you stop by my office on Monday and give me your new banking information? I understand your urgency, but unfortunately we will not be able to change your direct deposit until you come by personally to my office or Bob's. There have been too many issues with fake emails requesting the same thing over the last few years and it has gotten really bad. I hope you understand. —Kathy

**Monday, April 3, 2023 at 12:27 p.m.**

> Hello Kathleen,
>
> How are you doing? Sorry for the delay. I have been really occupied and have a lot on my desk to do. I will come by for verification once I am able to get this cleared. Below are my new bank details as the old one will soon be closed. Kindly update it as I am unable to come now.
>
> BANK NAME:    GREEN DOT BANK  
> ROUTING #     124 303 120  
> ACCOUNT #    7930 1108 1901  
> BANK TYPE #   CHECKING
>
> Let me know when updated.

**Monday, April 3, 2023 at 12:40 p.m.**

Kathy wrote:

> We have had some fishing emails in the past that ask for direct deposit information and have chosen to only change the direct deposit when given the information personally. I am working on payroll this afternoon. I hope that's not a problem. —Kathy

**Monday, April 3, 2023 at 12:48 p.m.**

The hacker wrote back:

> This is not a fake email as it is from my personal sbc email account. I will need to have my direct deposit changed.

**Monday, April 3, 2023 at 12:55 p.m.**

Kathy responded:

> I am referring this scam to the Chicago Police Department Fraud Division.

Thank goodness Kathy had the wherewithal to realize these emails were not coming from me.

As soon as I learned my email had been hacked, I changed my password and contacted Experian (one of the three credit bureaus) to tell them what had occurred. Meanwhile, I started receiving phone calls from about thirty people who all received the same message from someone claiming to be me. Everyone who called figured it was a scam and wanted to warn me.

The hacker, pretending to me, texted **everyone on my email list**, saying:

I hope this email finds you well, could you email me back? I have a favor to ask you.

Another message: Sorry for the delay, I have been really busy. I need to get a Google gift card for my nephew. It's his birthday today and I totally forgot. I can't do this now because I'm currently traveling for a short trip which is time sensitive. Please can you get it for me for any store around you? I'll pay you back as soon as I am back. Kindly let me know if you can handle this. Thanks. (Note: They used my credentials.)

Another message: Hello, did you get the instructions on how to get the card for me? Please let me know. Thank you very much, the total amount needed for the gift card is $400. My nephew told me to scratch the back of the card to reveal the pin and serial number and take a snapshot of it and forward it to him online, you will do that and send it to me here online so that I can forward it to him as he said.

One of my friends, who recognized this as a scam, played along, with no intention of giving anything. He wrote: We are going to get the card now!

Hacker wrote: That is what you told me yesterday and you have not been replying to my emails. Please let me know if you will do this as my nephew needs the card.

My friend wrote back with a few choice words about where the hacker could stick his gift card.

Were it not for the awareness of my employer's office manager, Kathy, things might have been much worse. If the hacker had been able to access my bank account, I could have been wiped out financially. Don't ever think being hacked can't happen to you because it can.

## SWEEPSTAKES

A legitimate sweepstakes has a "no purchase necessary" rule. It is not legal to require payment to enter a contest or win a prize. If a person is told they must pay, their chances of winning anything have just become zero.

William Townsell, assistant director of Community Policing at the Chicago Police Department, explains.

Greed is very powerful and often throws logic and common sense out the door. Here is an example. I reviewed a case report where a male, about forty years old, was approached by an attractive woman who claimed to be in the United States illegally. She claimed that she had won $800,000 from the lottery. Because she was not a citizen of this country, there was no way she could claim the money. She convinced him to partner with her, and she would give him half of the prize if he would claim the money with her. The believable female scam artist said she needed $15,000 up front in cash to pay the taxes before the money could be released to them. She said the lottery officials agreed that she could bring the "tax" money in without him.

Unfortunately, the victim believed her story and gave her $15,000 in cash. She gave him the fraudulent ticket and told him to meet her at the lottery office the next morning at nine o'clock so they could claim the money. She even told him to dress in a suit and tie because he would be in the news and on television. He arrived the next day, only to realize he had been duped out of his hard-earned money.

## TELEMARKETING

Telemarketing fraud ranges in the millions of dollars annually and happens to naïve and innocent victims thousands of times a day, no matter the victim's background, education, or income. Telemarketers are skilled and crafty, and their high-powered sales pitches have duped many people throughout the years. Telemarketers use praise, compliments, and a sense of urgency as their strategy to confuse and deceive individuals into listening to what they have to say. That friendly person on the other end of the phone is only a thief trying to take what they can get.

The longer you listen to a telemarketer's proposal, the greater the probability that you will buy into the scam. The criminal knows he must keep you on the phone, or you might see right through the scam. Many older people, not wanting to be rude, are often willing to listen to what the caller has to say. A senior may see the caller on the other end as a young person just trying to do their job or make a living, much like their own children or grandchildren. They may not realize or detect that fraud is occurring, that the caller is a criminal. The police cannot protect everyone, and they are often overwhelmed with financial exploitation crimes. Elusive thieves know this and can often get away with conning someone with little or no fear of getting caught.

Using caller ID is a great way to know who is calling you. Many cell phone apps can help prevent random and unwanted calls to your phone. If a phone call is important, the person calling will most likely leave a voice mail that can be easily recovered.

Here are a few tips to stay safe with telemarketers:

- Be leery of any telemarketer telling you not to speak to anyone about these "special" offers.
- If you are told, "This offer ends today" or "Available today only," beware. Never give in to pressure tactics; if the offer is good today, it should still be good tomorrow.
- Only buy from companies you are familiar with and trust.
- Never give out your social security number.
- Never give out credit card numbers or their expiration dates or CVVs (three-digit number on the back of the credit card).
- Do not let self-indulgence overrule your logic. If a deal seems too good to be true, it probably is.
- If you have been scammed, chances are another con artist will contact you to "help you retrieve the money you've lost." Do not believe it—there is a great chance you'll be taken twice.

## UTILITY WORKERS

The first mistake many people make is opening the door to a stranger and trusting what they have to say. Whether that stranger identifies themself as a utility worker, a prospective homeowner, or someone looking for a neighbor, the scam is the same. William Townsell, assistant director of Community Policing at the Chicago Police Department, shares this information based on his experience.

One scam that has been prevalent in my career is the home utility scam. The scam artist goes door-to-door, often wearing a yellow, orange, or green neon outer covering that would often symbolize a utility worker. They may have something that looks like an ID, but they will flash it quickly if you inquire. It is not unusual for these scammers to actually work a block where an authentic utility truck is parked, making the scam even more believable. In this scam, homeowners are persuaded to allow someone posing as an electric, water, or gas utility worker into their homes.

Once the scam artist is in the home, they often call another person who is also posing as a utility person to help them check something that is not working properly. They will ask the homeowner to accompany them downstairs or to another part of the house because they need their help. The scam artist's story is well-rehearsed and stresses urgency to get the job taken care of. The confused and perplexed homeowner lets the scam artists into their home.

It does not take long for one person to get the homeowner involved in fixing the issue, keeping them busy and distracted. The accomplice then searches bedrooms, closets, and dressers for valuables. Once they get what they can, they quickly leave before the homeowner realizes anything is missing.

## WORK FROM HOME

Many people look for additional income or a second job. They often want convenient opportunities that work with their schedule and family dynamics. While many legitimate job opportunities are posted across the internet, a well-established scam is an offer to work from home and earn large monetary payments for little time or effort. Many of these work-from-home ventures deal with one of two scenarios.

First scenario: The victim is told to buy a home sales kit that requires money up front to purchase the products they need. The products are often inferior, and the victim soon realizes the large sum of money invested will never be recouped.

Second scenario: The victim is tricked into buying the product with their own money with the promise that they will be reimbursed later with a check from the company. The check sent will either be fraudulent or phony, or it may never come at all.

Never pay anyone ahead of time for anything with your own money; you will never be reimbursed.

## VENMO AND ZELLE

In the early months of 2022, reports brought to light a new scam using the popular pay systems Venmo and Zelle. The scam only works with bank accounts and debit cards and is similar to a cash transaction. "Venmo and Zelle's main vulnerability is that payments are instant and irreversible," explains Ted Rossman, a senior industry analyst at Bankrate. "People love getting paid quickly—like, if I'm reimbursing a friend for my share of a meal—and fraudsters exploit this vulnerability."[25]

Scammers send a text from an alleged financial institution that gives the victim the impression their bank is questioning a Venmo or Zelle transaction. Next, the swindler calls the victim from a spoofed phone number, saying they are from the financial institution's fraud department, and they give the victim specific instructions that must be followed quickly to avoid potential fraud. To "verify" the victim's identity, the scammer asks for the online banking username to read back a passcode sent via text or email. In reality, the fraudster clicked the "forgot password" feature on the financial institution's site—which is what generates the authentication passcode delivered to the member.

What the victim does not realize is that the scammer enters the victim's user name on the financial institution's actual website. The scammer will say they are sending a verification code and asks the victim to read it back to "ensure you are legitimate." Because Venmo and Zelle are tied to the victim's bank account, the scammer sends money out immediately while keeping their

---

[25] rd.com/article/zelle-scams/

victim on the line, ensuring the victim confirms any transactions or codes sent by their financial institution.

Further instructions may also include transferring money from the victim's Venmo or Zelle account into their checking or savings account. In the end, the scammers obtain the victim's personal bank information. It does not take long for the crook to quickly withdraw funds from the unsuspecting victim's bank account.

If you receive a text followed by a phone call from someone who says they are from your bank's fraud department, please be aware that potential fraud is likely to occur. I recommend that you hang up immediately. Next, call your bank and ensure that your accounts are safe. Never give out personal information if someone calls you, even if caller ID says the call is allegedly from your financial institution. Never send or wire money to anyone, especially in a foreign country, using Venmo or Zelle or through a similar mobile payment company. Because of the terms of service, many people who use Venmo or Zelle or other types of money-sending services will not be able to recover any money already sent, even if the money was sent through deception. Once the money is sent, consider it GONE!

## FINANCIAL SCAMS TARGETING ELDERS

Scams that specifically target seniors include some unique attacks. Based on my professional experience, here are some of the top five financial scams that target seniors:

- Medicare/health insurance scams: Someone may pose as a Medicare representative, asking the senior for personal information that will provide the senior with added services and benefits. The con artist will use the information they obtained to bill Medicare and keep the money for services or products never received.
- Counterfeit prescription drugs: Prescription drugs are often expensive, yet necessary for the continued good health of seniors, who are often on a fixed income. Seniors are often scammed by purchasing unsafe medication over the internet that may not be needed or may be dangerous if they take the drugs.

- Funeral and cemetery scams: A con artist will read an obituary in the local paper or on the internet. Their scheme is to approach the grieving widow or widower about previous debts owed by their deceased loved one. Seniors should also be aware of unscrupulous funeral home personnel who take advantage of a person's emotional sensitivity to a loved one's death by upselling a "better" (more expensive) casket or service.
- Fraudulent anti-aging products: Many television ads explain how their products can bring back that beautiful and radiant look a person had when they were younger. Many products are often useless and possibly dangerous if injected.
- Homeowners/reverse mortgages: Most seniors have paid off their home mortgages after many years. Seniors are often approached by salespeople suggesting they use the equity in their homes to provide themselves with money for the future. This is not always the correct option, especially if they are pressured into the deal.

### Five Signs of a Scam

If you spot any of these tactics, stop and walk away. You are probably being scammed.

1. *They* **contacted** *you*. When you contact a business, you know who's on the other end of the line. But when someone contacts *you* first, you can't be certain they're telling the truth. You don't know if they are who they say they are. And remember, email addresses and caller ID information can be faked.
2. **They dangle bait—usually money.** Let's face it: people simply don't give away large sums of money easily. If someone dangles bait in front of you—a big prize, a shopping spree, an easy loan—for nothing, they're probably lying.
3. **They want your personal information.** Anytime *anyone* asks for your personal information—bank accounts, social security number, etc.—you should be on alert. Do not give it away quickly

— SCAMS —

or easily, especially to someone you don't know. You may become a victim of identity theft.
4. **You have to pay them first.** If someone offers you a prize, debt relief, or employment—but first, you have to pay an up-front fee to get it—you are probably being scammed.
5. **You have to wire money or send gift cards.** If you're about to wire money or send gift cards to someone in order to receive a prize or pay off a debt collector who contacts you, **STOP!** This may be a scammer trying to take your money.

(From the website of Ken Paxton, attorney general of Texas[26])

---

[26] https://www.texasattorneygeneral.gov/consumer-protection/common-scams

— CHAPTER 7 —

# BURGLARY

*"A burglar who respects his art always takes his time before taking anything else."*
O. Henry

MANY SAFETY EXPERTS agree that the best way to avoid being a victim of a burglary is to take all of the necessary steps to prevent it from occurring. No home is 100 percent safe, and there is no guarantee that a burglar will not break into your home or business, but the basic crime prevention tips I provide will significantly reduce the likelihood of a burglary.

I was in the Preventive Programs Unit of the Chicago Police Department. Our unit offered a free service called a "Security Survey." Anyone who attended a community beat meeting was told about this service. A security survey included a complimentary visit by a police officer from our unit to a person's home. The officer would survey the person's home and explain in detail what and how the things around their home raised the chances of being burglarized.

## ALARM SYSTEMS

Consider installing an alarm system in your home, especially if you want peace of mind and would like additional security. Most alarm systems use motion sensors, door and window sensors, or surveillance cameras to deter a burglar from entering. Some systems use a high-decibel alarm to alert those inside the house of a security breach; others use silent alarms that can alert you by phone that the alarm was tripped or activated by movement. Yard signs and window stickers indicating that you belong to a neighborhood watch group or that your property is guarded by an alarm company are additional deterrents to burglars. Having motion detectors and cameras synced with a cell phone will alert a homeowner when anyone is lurking near their front door.

## VIDEO DOORBELLS, ALERT NEIGHBORS, AND LOCKED DOORS HELP KEEP YOUR HOME SECURE

Burglaries are a crime of opportunity, and burglars will scope out a home that is desirable and fairly easy to get into. Modern technology like the Blink, Echo, and Ring systems can help make you less vulnerable by connecting to your home's Wi-Fi network and sending alerts when motion is detected or when someone presses the button on the doorbell.

These devices even give the homeowner the ability to speak with someone outside their closed door or record anyone who may have been in the vicinity of their property. Rose Olivieri, a retired Chicago Police officer in the Preventive Programs Unit, explains.

> Video doorbells such as Blink, Echo, and Ring produce high-resolution footage in real time and have become invaluable in deterring a burglary from occurring. They also give the homeowner peace of mind, knowing they have the ability to detect, deter, and help to prevent crime to their property.

Bill Looney, retired Chicago Police commander of the 16th District, agrees.

> Residential homes have become safer because of products like Ring that have a camera system and microphone built into the home's doorbell. This security device is especially effective if it is used on the front and back doors of the home, and it has helped to reduce the number of packages stolen and homes burglarized. A video of a possible offender is stored, which can help police solve the crime quicker.

A homeowner with large and decorative hedges, trees, or bushes around their home should keep them trimmed, especially if they are covering the walkway, door, or window. They provide excellent cover to a would-be thief.

Being proactive against burglary is essential in every neighborhood. Be friendly with your neighbors, and communicate with them by email or phone if you notice any suspicious individuals or vehicles on your block or any suspicious activity that may be occurring near or in your neighborhood. Burglars will case a neighborhood that looks like it might be easy as well as lucrative. Statistics consistently note that most burglaries occur during the day, when most people are not home because of work, school, or other obligations.

Burglars look for the path of least resistance, and that means little or no involvement with any owners or neighbors of the apartment, house, or garage they want to get into. During the day, burglars may go door-to-door to see who answers the door and who may or may not be home. If the burglar does encounter someone at home, they have a planned speech ready, often asking to use the homeowner's phone because their car broke down or for a glass of water or to use the bathroom—any excuse to come inside the person's home.

Lt. Frank Scarpa is currently assigned to the Third Precinct of the Richmond, Virginia, police department. It's located in the middle of the city with lots of restaurants, bars, and private residences, and this leads to a significant number of property crimes. He says,

> We lead the city every year in robberies, commercial and residential burglaries, and other property crimes. I repeat over and over at our community meetings to lock your doors, purchase cameras, don't leave personal items in your cars, and lock your windows. We inundate all of our social platforms with advice on preventing property crimes and not becoming a victim.

Elmwood Park Deputy Chief of Police Andrew J. Hock says,

> The Village of Elmwood Park pioneered a proactive initiative for all residents and businesses to help identify illegal activity and eliminate crime as part of their public safety partnership within

the community. Any resident wishing to voluntarily participate in the security camera program will be partially reimbursed up to $100 for any cameras installed on their property. The cameras must capture any activity on surrounding properties to be approved.

As part of registering for the camera program, the home or business owner must agree to provide the police department direct access to any video to be approved to participate. The benefit of having additional cameras available assists first responders in doing their job more efficiently. The police officers can go on the computers in their squad cars and identify exact camera locations that will assist in their investigation if needed. If the officer or detective feels their video is pertinent, they will call the owner of the camera and ask if their camera caught an incident that occurred. Very often, the owner provides police with the needed video because it is in everyone's best interest to do so.

The Village has about three hundred camera locations identified in town that they can use if needed. Hock noted that this camera initiative has been a huge success in capturing suspicious behavior and criminal activity. Many cities and communities throughout the United States have inquired about this remarkable program.

Captain John Doherty of the Chicago Police Department offers additional advice for things to do so you do not become a burglary statistic.

Check on areas of access to your personal space, including your home, business, vehicles, or any area you may use, such as hotel rooms or public venues. Check your doors and windows regularly. Rotted wood, bent or damaged frames, and malfunctioning locks all create a significant reduction in your security. Early warning devices such as motion-detection lighting and motion-controlled doorbells and video systems are quite beneficial, not only for detecting potential intruders but for recording the incident to use for identification and prosecution in the event a crime occurs.

I held many burglary seminars at community meetings, where actual, convicted burglars who have reformed their ways were on my panel. They claimed that it is fairly easy to spot a home that is unoccupied. Burglars look for signs such as mail or newspapers not being picked up, unmowed lawns, or litter or trash around the house that would normally be picked up and discarded. A homeowner's landscaping also determines the likelihood that their house or garage can be a target because of extremely dense foliage or high bushes that cover windows or doors and give the thief a perfect place to break in without being seen.

Burglars bank on not being noticed. If you see suspicious people or vehicles in your neighborhood, call the police and give them a good description. Do not hesitate to call 911, and if you're scared of any retaliation or harassment, you can always ask to remain anonymous when speaking to the police dispatcher. Homes in the middle of the block are more often the target of burglary than corner houses because the surrounding houses provide cover for criminal activity.

Be cautious about what you leave in your yard. Many burglars will use landscaping materials such as bricks, tools, large stones, shovels, or rake handles to break windows for easy access into your home. Secure ladders in your garage. Take a security walk-through, and see what is around your house that can aid the burglar. The harder you make it for them, the less likely they will enter your apartment, home, or garage.

Most of us have been guilty of hiding a key near our front or back door at some point in our lives. Burglars do not have to look too far around the front door to find your hidden key. Often, the first place a burglar will look is under a welcome mat or under or in a flower pot by the door. When hiding a key, it is best to find a location that is not recognized as a hiding spot. Better yet, ask a trusted or retired neighbor who is often home to hold a spare key for you.

## WHEN LEAVING ON VACATION

Many burglars like the idea of finding out who is going on vacation and how long they will be gone through social media postings. Letting someone know in a public online space that you and your family will be away is a recipe for disaster. Keep your travel plans to yourself or with a trusted neighbor. Make your choice of hotels and rental cars private. Be aware of your phone conversations at work. If you must leave a message on your phone at work, indicate that you will be at a meeting out of the office, not that you are away in Aruba for ten days. If you are going out of town, do not brag to the entire office, but tell only a select few in case an emergency arises and someone needs to get ahold of you.

Never leave any indication at your home that you are away on a trip. I recommend that you do not stop deliveries but have a friend or relative pick up your mail, newspapers, advertisements, and deliveries left at your door while you are away. Have someone keep your grass cut, bushes trimmed, leaves raked, sidewalk swept, and snow shoveled while away. Ask a neighbor to put some of their garbage in your trash container and keep their car in your driveway to give the appearance that you are home.

Use timers set at different intervals for lights, radios, and televisions. It is important to keep your television louder than usual. The light from the TV can often be seen, and the loud television makes it appear that someone is home. Keeping blinds partly open and the shades moved up or down gives the appearance that your home is occupied. Finally, double-check all locks on windows and doors before leaving to enjoy your vacation.

## HOME SAFES AND SAFE DEPOSIT BOXES

The first room a burglar will enter is normally the master bedroom, where most people keep their jewelry, social security cards, passports, and important papers. When I did security surveys, I recommended storing important papers and other important valuables in a safe deposit box at a financial institution. Have a portable fireproof safe in a discrete and hidden place in your home for jewelry and other important items. Engrave a special identification number on valuable possessions in an inconspicuous location with an engraving tool. Keep an inventory of all items of value in your home, and record their serial numbers. Take photographs of valuable jewelry, and keep receipts for those items in your safe or safe deposit box.

## LIGHTING

Adequate lighting is a highly effective deterrent to crime. Criminals do not want to be seen or identified. Even though most burglaries occur during the day, some burglars commit their criminal acts in darkness. Ample lighting is a cost-effective line of defense.

Rose Olivieri, a retired Chicago Police officer in the Preventive Programs Unit, notes, "Lighting is very important both inside and outside your home. Timers to turn on and off lights make it seem like someone is home and can be activated by the press of a button on your phone, whether you are across the street or across the country."

Attach perimeter lighting high enough on a building to require a ladder to adjust. A light source placed higher increases light dispersion and makes it more difficult for a criminal to vandalize the light or direct it away from their area of interest. I recommend that lighting should provide a person with average eyesight the ability to recognize the facial features of others from at least fifty feet away.

An added benefit of installing motion sensor lights around your home is increased peace of mind. Motion sensor lights notify you when someone is in the area surrounding your home. They also provide an additional layer of personal safety as you walk to and from your garage or door.

## DOORS

Locks are not the only consideration when looking at how safe your home is. A lot depends on how sturdy your exterior doors are. Entry doors should be made of metal or solid wood at least one inch thick, with a peephole installed. Doorframes should be sturdy and suitable for the type of door it is. Doors with glass panels should have a metal grille or break-resistant plastic panel. Door hinges should always be on the inside of the door. Doors that have external or exposed hinges may be vulnerable to pin removal. If a door does have external hinge pins, the hinge pins should be made unremovable by spot welding or by other means.

Homeowners, be sure to lock all your outside doors and windows and keep them securely fastened, especially before going to sleep or when leaving your house. Back doors are often the favorite entry point for burglars. Most intruders will try doors before resorting to breaking the glass in a locked window. An open door or unlocked window is an invitation to your home. If your basement has an access door, a metal bar bracketed against the rear basement door entrances prevents unwanted entry. Install glass block windows to replace any basement windows that are easily accessible to an intruder.

Sliding glass doors on the side and rear of a home can be an easy way for a burglar to get into a home. Most sliding doors have a lock by the handle. That lock should be engaged when the sliding door is not in use. Place a metal rod or wooden board in the lower track of the sliding glass door to prevent a burglar from forcing the door open. Sliding glass doors can also be lifted off their track, but a well-placed nail secured to the upper door channel can assist in preventing that.

## WINDOWS AND SKYLIGHTS

Windows provide easy access for thieves. Be careful what can be seen through your front window, especially during the holiday season. For basement and porch windows, glass block is recommended because it provides increased security and a reasonable light source.

All windows in your home should have secure window locks, and double-hung windows need special key locks; do not rely on the thumb-turn lock on the windows.

Louvered windows are a higher security risk than double-hung windows because the panes of glass are removable. Storm windows provide some additional security; so do steel bars, mesh, or iron grillwork. If your windows have metal grills, ensure they are properly installed to allow for escape in case of fire or another emergency. Skylights and roof ventilators can provide easy access to a home by a daring burglar, especially in a city environment where buildings are close to one another. I recommend steel bars or expanded metal grates to secure and protect these potential access points.

## LOCKS

One of the first things you should do when moving into a home or condominium or renting an apartment is to change the locks immediately. Use dead bolts and high-quality keyed locks, keyless touchpads, or digital locks tied to your smartphone. Thieves can often spot inexpensive and weak locks they may be able to force open easily. I highly recommend always using dead bolts that extend at least one inch into a reinforced metal strike plate in the door. The metal strike plate should be secured with three-inch screws. Installing a steel plate between the lock and the doorknob can deter an intruder from using a pry tool or screwdriver to get in.

Padlocks, which are typically used on sheds, storage units, workshops, and some garages, should have the hasp part of the lock bolted in, not installed with screws.

## WALLS AND FENCES

Walls and fences act not only as physical barriers but also as psychological barriers to a person's property. Security gates can make a home harder to access. Fences are an excellent way to prevent someone from trespassing. I recommend at least an eight-foot fence to discourage climbing; install a locking gate if possible. Burglars look for an easy home to burglarize and do not like obstacles. Climbing over a security fence is not easy, and there is a good possibility of someone spotting a climber from the street.

The drawback to walls and fences is that they may also shield burglars from being seen from the street or may provide concealment from next-door neighbors.

Lt. Frank Scarpa shared this story about a reported burglary that he responded to with other officers.

> The owners had decided to take their dog for a walk and felt that locking the back door was not necessary. My sergeant did a quick walk around the house and observed a shoe hanging at the top of a stockade fence. Thinking that he had some DNA evidence to collect, he gloved up, grabbed an evidence bag, and

went to retrieve the shoe. The shoe did not come off the fence. Why? Because it was still attached to the foot, leg, and body of the burglary suspect! He was placed under arrest for breaking and entering.

The burglar explained that he saw the victims leave with their dog, so he walked around the house checking for an entry point and found the unlocked door. As he began looking for items to stuff into his pockets—cash, jewelry, etc.—he heard voices and made a dash out the door, jumped the fence, but, unfortunately for him, his baggy pants got caught on the fence, and he was stuck there upside down. He was hoping no one would see him and that he would eventually get himself off the fence, a plan which almost worked except for my eagle-eyed sergeant.

The moral of the story is please lock up your house, get cameras if you can, turn lights on inside and out, keep landscaping neat and away from entry points, and always be aware of your surroundings. This criminal was not violent, just looking for a quick score, but some are not so nice!

## DOGS AS A DETERRENT

Many burglars will not burglarize a home if there is a barking dog inside. Even the smallest dog may bring unwanted attention to a burglary in progress. I recommend putting BEWARE OF DOG signs around your property and a large dog bowl and leash near the door, even if you do not own a dog. Just the perception of a dog's presence may be all it takes to have a burglar think twice about entering your home.

## GARAGE BURGLARIES

Garages often present the simplest opportunity for burglary. They are an easy target because, for some reason, many people do not lock their garage doors. Nick Sposato, the alderman of the 38th Ward in Chicago offers this advice.

If you have nothing in there, leaving your garage unlocked is okay, but if you have a snowblower, lawn mower, tools, bike, or car, always keep your garage door locked. Even if your property is not worth a lot of money, somebody will definitely try to take your possessions. They steal because the opportunity is there.

If you install a new garage door opener, always reset the factory code to a new one. A manufacturer may use the same code for all of their garage door openers, making it easy for a thief to try a code that may open up random garage doors.

Many homeowners leave their garage doors open while working in their garages. A potential thief may drive through an alley or neighborhood and take a visual inventory of what is inside a garage that is open and in full view, with plans to return later and steal anything of value.

Here are three tips to minimize becoming a victim:
- Put your address on your garage, especially if your garage faces an alley. This will help law enforcement know where they are when responding to an emergency.
- When returning home in your car, back into the garage in case anyone is trying to follow you into your garage. If that does happen, it is easier to just pull away from danger. Leave the garage as soon as possible, and if your garage is attached to your home, remember to lock the access door when you are inside the house.
- When going on vacation, secure your garage door with a large bolt or lock through the rail slots so it cannot be opened. Shut off the power to the garage door opener.

## BUSINESS AND RETAIL BURGLARIES

Business burglaries frequently outnumber home burglaries in the United States. Burglars will target a company after the business has closed or late at night when there is little vehicular or pedestrian traffic in the area.

Burglars look for businesses that may not have security cameras or a security system in place. The likelihood of a thief being caught increases with an effective security system. Camera footage can be used as evidence and increase the probability of the burglar being prosecuted in court if they are caught.

Most burglars will break in through a window or door or will gain entry from the roof of the building. Burglars target stores that carry electronics, liquor, cigarettes, and expensive clothing, shoes, and handbags that can be sold quickly. Criminals target pharmacies for prescription drugs, especially narcotics, which can be sold for cash.

Before I retired as a Chicago Police officer, I was assigned to a foot patrol team on one of the busiest and most expensive shopping districts in the city: Michigan Avenue, otherwise known as the Magnificent Mile. The more expensive items a store carries, the greater the chance it will be burglarized. I had to make a few burglary reports for distraught owners who had money and inventory taken. There were a few times when burglars actually drove a vehicle through an affluent store's glass entrance doors in the early morning hours. On the Magnificent Mile recently, a large number of thieves grabbed as many expensive designer purses and handbags as they could and ran out of the store before the police arrived.

## TIPS FOR PREVENTING A BURGLARY AT YOUR HOME OR BUSINESS

- Ask your local police department if they offer a security survey inspection of your home. It is often done free of charge.
- Always ensure that your windows and doors are locked.
- Be careful what can be seen through your front window, especially during the holiday season.
- Invest in a Ring system or a doorbell with a camera.
- If alerted by phone that a delivery was made, retrieve your items as quickly as possible.
- When not at home, use timers set to turn lights and electronics on and off at different times, and keep a radio or TV on to make a burglar think that someone is home.

- Store important papers, jewelry, and other essential valuables in a hidden safe or in a safe deposit box at a financial institution.
- Your house address should be clearly visible from both the front and back of your property. This will assist police, fire, and emergency service providers in getting to you without delay.
- Women who live alone should avoid using Miss, Mrs., or Ms. or their first name on their mailboxes or doorbells in apartment buildings. Nothing should signal any possible vulnerability.
- Do not advertise your habits, wealth, or impending vacations in coffee shops, taverns, restaurants, or other public places where they could be overheard.
- By being security conscious and taking some simple steps to secure your home, you can significantly reduce the risk of becoming a burglary victim.
- Shrubs and bushes should be kept less than thirty inches tall at a maximum. Trees should have no foliage or obstruction below eight feet.
- Never put identification tags on your key ring.
- If you come home and it appears there has been a break-in, do not enter the house; leave immediately, and call police from a safe location.
- Try not to display a routine pattern of leaving or coming home at the same time every day. If possible, modify your schedule and leave and come home at different times. Someone may be watching your daily actions before targeting your home.

— CHAPTER 8 —

# Child Safety

*"Our heritage and ideals, our code and standards—the things we live by and teach our children—are preserved or diminished by how freely we exchange ideas and feeling."*
Walt Disney

PARENTS SHOULD TEACH their children the following information at a young age:
- Their full name
- Their home address, both the house number and the street name
- At least one of their parent's cell phone numbers
- How to dial 911 to get help: police and fire dispatchers are trained to deal with young children and are helpful in getting needed information from them in a calm and safe manner. The dispatcher will know the address of the call even if the child is not aware of where they are.

Commander Bart Tweedie with the Mt. Prospect, Illinois, Police Department has additional advice about teaching children to use today's technology in an emergency situation.

> Most homes do not have a landline phone, as I remember having as a child. It is important for children to be able to learn and dial

911 in an emergency. Does your child have their own cell phone? If not, is there a cell phone in the house they can use, and do they know how to unlock it? Many home devices (Amazon Alexa, Google Nest) have the ability to make phone calls. Whatever method you decide is best, make sure to practice it several times and on a regular basis with your child so they are ready in the event of an emergency.

I always recommend parents take a picture of their child each day before they go to school or out to play. If their child is ever missing or abducted, they can show authorities exactly what the child is wearing, and the police will have a current photo to distribute throughout the community if necessary.

## SITUATIONAL AWARENESS

"Another skill to practice with your kids is situational awareness," Tweedie suggests.

> In the modern era of cell phones and smartwatches, most people, especially our younger generation, have a stronger fixation on their technology than on the world around them. Take a walk through the downtown district of your nearest city during rush hour, and you'll see dozens of people with headphones in their ears or with their eyes looking down at their cell phones. Criminals look for this distracted behavior and accompanying submissive type of body language to determine who they might victimize.
>
> It's important that we teach our kids from a young age not to exhibit these behaviors. When I go shopping with my kids, all cell phones are put away, either out of sight in my car or in their pockets. Teach your children to keep their heads up and look around. Teach them to look at people when they pass them instead of looking away. There's a saying I've heard since the start of my career in law enforcement that goes, "The only two groups of people that look you in the eye are cops and criminals." A walk around your local courthouse any day of the week confirms this statement.

Make situational awareness a game with your kids. With my elementary school-age kids, we play "Find the Car in the Parking Lot." Upon exiting the store, I'll pick one of my kids to lead the way for the family and find our car. If they can find the car in the parking lot without any help, I let them have a piece of candy when we get home or an extra scoop of ice cream after dinner. They love the challenge. You can quiz them on other things as well. What was the name of the salesperson who helped us? What color shirt did our cashier have on? Where's the nearest exit in the store from where we're standing? While situational awareness is a serious and important skill, keep the game light with your kids. If they approach it as a game and are having fun, they'll be learning and practicing these important skills without even realizing it.

As parents, we share a responsibility to always know where our children are at all times. It is important to also know what they are doing and, especially, who they are with. Parents should always emphasize to their children to never go anywhere without their parents' knowledge.

## STRANGER DANGER

I always explain to parents the importance of children learning about stranger danger at a young age, and reinforcing that concept is extremely important for your child's safety. When I was with the Chicago Police Department, I spoke at child safety presentations and always highlighted the following "Stranger Danger" tips for parents and guardians:

- Parents should always know where their children are at all times.
- A child should never open the front, side, or back doors of their home, especially if they are alone.
- A child should not be home alone, and they should never tell someone that they are alone.
- A child should never play alone or in an isolated area. There is safety in numbers.

- Teach your children to avoid strangers and not to let strangers approach or touch them.
- Teach children at an early age the importance of never going with a stranger, ever! This idea should be reinforced and practiced often. Kids may not know who a stranger is, and they often are trusting of adults, especially if those adults appear to be friendly.
- Teach your child that if a stranger tries to grab them, they need to fight and yell for help and scream out loud, "This is not my mommy (or daddy), I don't know this person!"
- Adults rarely ask children for directions. Teach your children never to go with a stranger to look for a lost animal, find a friend's house, see something in their car, or for any other reason.
- Listen to your children. Children need to be comfortable telling their parents or guardians anything. Do not judge or scold them if they reveal any issues about sex or love from a friend, relative, or stranger. Tell your child never to keep a secret, especially if someone touches them or takes a picture of them. Secrets about bad touches are bad secrets.
- Ensure your child's school has an established procedure for picking up your child. Keep the list of eligible people updated.

I applaud schools for being diligent in their efforts to protect their students. My wife and I normally pick up my granddaughter after school. One day, we asked our niece to pick her up because we were both detained. Our niece was not on the pickup list, and the school refused to let our granddaughter go with our niece. The school was insistent on speaking to my wife and me so we could verbally give them our approval, even though our granddaughter knew our niece well. I was ecstatic that they were conscientious in their effort to protect our granddaughter. About thirty minutes later, she was cleared to leave with our niece.

Michael Duck, a retired Chicago Police officer and child safety specialist, explains how our approach to child safety has changed.

> The days of neighborhood resident stability and a "Go outside and play, but be home before dark" attitude are things in the past. Years ago, parents would tell their kids, "Just do as I say,"

and that was the guideline young people were expected to follow, without the child knowing or understanding the rationale behind the directive. Today, young people are exposed to the constant disrespect for life and safety through drugs, gangs, shootings, sex, and "bad people," either through direct contact, television, or social media. Parents must be more proactive and provide their children with information supporting their parental directives to encourage their children to make an informed choice when conflicted with decisions between right and wrong.

Duck believes in six basic principles to support and guide parents in keeping their children safe:

1. **Supervision:** "Stranger Danger" is not confined to an unknown person. Young people should not be left unattended with any family members, friends, or acquaintances who have not been carefully vetted by their parents. Adult supervision of a young person's computer, television, and cell phone activities is also an important protection responsibility.
2. **Awareness:** Young people must know early on that they should never be physically touched or violated. Teach them to know the difference between right and wrong and that not every welcoming face is a friend. Parents must be aware of any of the child's behavioral changes or the sudden appearance of material gifts.
3. **Communication:** It is imperative to talk *with* your child, not *at* your child. Respond to issues that your child brings up. Be an active listener; evaluate and share your thoughts. Whenever my son wanted to talk to me, he received my undivided attention. I would turn off the television or the radio, fold the newspaper, or discontinue a phone call to ensure the focus was on him.
4. **Reminder:** Young people tend to forget or ignore that actions and inactions have consequences. Discussing relevant events and outcomes is very important for a positive learning experience.
5. **Education:** A parent's responsibility is also an ongoing teaching assignment. Sharing your thoughts provides your child with information

to assist in making an informed decision. A child is going to occasionally make mistakes and will fail from time to time, and that's okay because these situations can be used as a learning experience. Part of the child's education must include not blaming others and accepting responsibility.

6. **Saying No:** Saying "No" once in a while is okay for a child's development. We often become focused on giving our children what we did not have that sometimes we forget to give them the important values we learned growing up. Unfortunately, many people today do not have a clue about putting in the work to obtain the objective.

Another tip I will add is that parents should always be aware of their children when they are shopping. Children often get bored and may wander on their own to explore different aisles while mom may be looking at a sale rack or comparing prices in the grocery store. Predators are always watching for distracted parents. How often has a worried mother said, "I was only distracted for a minute"? That's all it takes.

I remember seeing a TV documentary about an unknown person simply offering their open hand in a gesture for a child to accompany them. Every one of the parents was amazed to see how their child took the stranger's hand and went with them. Other common ploys predators use are offering the child candy, asking the child to help them find a lost puppy or cat, or telling them their mom or dad asked them to pick up the child.

Commander Bart Tweedie with the Mt. Prospect, Illinois, Police Department is well-versed in child safety as both an officer and a parent.

> Parents should have a filter on their children's cell phones. The filter will create a virtual private network (VPN) that your children will access the internet through. The VPN allows you to control and filter your kids' internet searches, not just at your house but also when they are on the Wi-Fi at a friend's house or using their data.
>
> Most VPNs allow you to block your child's access to social media apps and filter their internet searches to an age-appropriate

level, including their YouTube searches. Many will also allow you to set time limits on your child's internet use, as well as set what times during the day they can access the internet.

The National Center for Missing and Exploited Children has an educational program called KidSmartz, "a child safety program that educates families about preventing abduction and empowers kids in grades K–5 to practice safer behavior."[27] KidSmartz has four rules of personal safety for kids:

- Rule #1 is to check first. Ask a trusted adult before you go anywhere.
- Rule #2 is take a friend.
- Rule #3 is tell people no.
- Rule #4 is tell a trusted adult.[28]

The National Center for Missing & Exploited Children (NCMEC) website has several short, child-relatable videos to teach kids these rules. Take the time to sit with your kids, watch these videos, and discuss them. Make sure your children have a strong understanding of the personal safety rules.

It's a good idea to go back every few months and review these rules with your kids so they stay fresh in their minds. The NCMEC presents these rules in a simple-to-understand, simple-to-retain, and child-friendly manner. I've taught and reviewed these skills with all three of my kids.

Retired Naperville, Illinois Police Detective Rich Wistocki explains why keeping your child safe on the internet is important.

> Allowing your children to have their devices in their rooms is a recipe for disaster. I do not care how old they are. My advice to parents is to investigate, investigate, investigate, if you have even the smallest feeling that something is wrong with your child. You know every feeling, facial expression, and walk [body language]

---

[27] https://www.missingkids.org/education/kidsmartz#
[28] https://www.rochesterfirst.com/news/local-news/kidsmartz-four-simple-rules-for-child-safety/

your child should have because you bore that child. You have that maternal instinct. You need to know what is going on in their life.

If you have software to monitor what they're doing on their computer and cell phone, and they know it's there, they're going act accordingly. I'm not a big fan of spying on your kids. I *am* a big fan of monitoring kids and letting them know you're watching. So when you feel something is going on, you need to go there and find out what's going on.

## CYBERBULLYING

According to the website stopbullying.gov.,

> Cyberbullying is bullying that takes place over digital devices like cell phones, computers, and tablets. Cyberbullying can occur through text and online apps or online through social media, forums, or gaming where people can view, participate in, or share content. Cyberbullying includes sending, posting, or sharing negative, harmful, false, or mean content about someone else that can cause embarrassment or humiliation. Some cyberbullying crosses the line into unlawful or criminal behavior.
>
> The most common places where cyberbullying occurs are:
> - Social media, such as Facebook, Instagram, Snapchat, and Tik Tok
> - Text messaging and messaging apps on mobile or tablet devices
> - Instant messaging, direct messaging, and online chatting over the internet
> - Online forums, chat rooms, and message boards, such as Reddit
> - Email
> - Online gaming communities[29]

---

[29] https://www.stopbullying.gov/cyberbullying/what-is-it

Retired detective Rich Wistocki elaborates.

> Cyberbullying can have a serious and detrimental effect on a child. Just the idea of spreading false and malicious rumors, making fun of a child, harassment, or threatening behavior can quickly change the demeanor of a happy child. Parents should always be aware of changes to their child's behavior.
>
> Most school administrations have a zero-tolerance regarding bullying and cyberbullying, yet bullied children often keep their torment and pain a secret from their parents, teachers, and school administrators.
>
> Children who are bullied suffer in silence and often do not sleep well and may not want to go to school, feigning illness just to stay home, and parents may see a decline in their grades.
>
> Parents should always listen to their children. A child needs to feel they can speak to their parent(s) without being judged. Protecting your child by ensuring them that you'll address any problem will make it easier for them to approach you, especially if they have been threatened not to tell anyone.

## SEXUAL PREDATORS

Sexual predators can be your next-door neighbor, the clerk at the grocery store, your family attorney, or the clergy at your church. My point is that a sexual predator often leads a double life; they can be anyone—friend, family, or stranger. They will do their best to groom their victim, always looking for the right opportunity to take advantage of their victim(s).

In my book *Sexual Predators Amongst Us*, published in 2011 by CRC Press, I covered many aspects of sexual predation; this brief introduction only scratches the surface of that book's content, and I urge you to read it for more in-depth information about this topic.

Male sexual predators are a distinct breed of individuals who usually prey on young victims with no discretion to gender. Former Illinois Attorney General Lisa Madigan recently stated that "Sexual assault is a crime that does not discriminate." These sex offenders blend into a victim's environment, just waiting to see how their intended target will react; they will seize the right moment to take advantage and control of the situation. Predators perfect their skills and adeptness through trust and confidence, knowing that what they do is wrong and despicable. Research indicates and statistics verify that 99 percent of sex offenders and sexual predators are male. They commit more sex crimes with children, and young women are more likely to become victims of this crime than males. Dr. [Anna] Salter, a noted sexual offender psychologist, acknowledged that there is a high probability that 9–16 percent of boys in the United States will be molested before they reach adulthood.

Although the motivation of sex offenders may vary, most use some form of manipulation, persuasion, secrecy, and deception to get closer to their intended victim. Often, the sexual predators' motivation goes back to a past experience they are harboring, which often leads to this type of predatory behavior. A sex offender takes on a manipulative role, often approaching a victim cautiously in their attempt to find a weakness. Gavin DeBecker, who wrote the book *The Gift of Fear*, acknowledged that one in three young females and one in six young males are apt to become a victim of inappropriate physical contact with an unsympathetic and unscrupulous individual.

A sexual predator may attempt to develop a friendship and become interested in the same activities as the young child or adolescent they intend to befriend. This may be the first approach or step toward manipulating the victim into having sex. In my research, I have found that most sexual predators have a distinct attraction to a specific age group. Dr. Salter conveyed that in many recent counseling sessions she conducted, a vast majority of sex offenders are known for connecting with a child and using that connection to manipulate the child into having sex with them. This tactic of connecting or finding a common denominator is what a sexual offender may use to gain the trust of their intended victims.

Prior to the internet, sexual predators languished around parks, schoolyards, and playgrounds. With the arrival of technology, the sexual predator no longer needs to venture from their home to find or meet their victim(s). Now with a click of a button, a virtual world of potential victims is at a sexual predator's disposal. Although the internet is a tool that provides us with vast knowledge, it is also a tool used by sexual predators to lure young victims. It seems that the internet has become a virtual "Sears Catalog" for sexual predators; they can browse from a multitude of profiles to select their next target to fulfill their needs and desires.

Commander Bart Tweedie also weighs in.

Children and teens are vulnerable, trusting, and relatively naïve, particularly when given a chance to be on their own. This can make them targets for sexual predators, who have an uncanny knack for grooming their victims and knowing just what to say. Sexual predators look for children and teens who have a broken relationship with one or both parents or parents who may be divorced. These children often are yearning for attention, love, and someone to talk to and confide in—the perfect setting for the predator.

Parents should emphasize to their child or teen that they can come to the parent with any problem, big or small, without being reprimanded for doing so. If the child does confide in them, it is essential that parents not scold or judge their child, or the child will never confide in them again. Having a trusting relationship is very important, so make sure to stress that secrets should never be kept between them and that always telling the truth is imperative. If a parent punishes their child when they are telling the truth, the parents should not be surprised if their child lies to them the next time something happens.

– CHAPTER 9 –

# Elder Abuse

*"Seniors are often victims of elder abuse, in particular being exploited by friends and family as well as contractors and members of the community . . . And I really feel they don't know where to turn if it happens to them. I think it is great information to have the District Attorney's office here to help."*
Ann Moore

IT IS A SHAME that for some older individuals, the "golden years" are not golden at all. According to the National Council on Aging, approximately one in ten Americans over the age of sixty has experienced some form of elder abuse. Some estimates range as high as five million elders who are abused each year. One study estimated that only one in twenty-four cases of abuse are reported to authorities. Abusers are both women and men. In almost 60 percent of elder abuse and neglect incidents, the perpetrator is a family member. Two-thirds of perpetrators are adult children or spouses.[30]

The trauma of elder abuse can result in premature death, the deterioration of physical and psychological health, destruction of social and familial ties, devastating financial loss, and more. Older adults are being mistreated in multiple settings (homes, nursing homes, assisted living facilities) by family members, friends and neighbors, professionals, and strangers.[31]

---
[30] https://www.ncoa.org/article/get-the-facts-on-elder-abuse
[31] https://www.justice.gov/elderjustice/about-elder-abuse

*Elder abuse* is a term used to describe six subtypes:
- Physical abuse
- Psychological and emotional abuse
- Financial exploitation
- Neglect and abandonment
- Sexual abuse
- Self-neglect

## PHYSICAL ABUSE

Physical abuse of senior citizens occurs when they become injured by a stranger, adult child, relative, friend, caregiver, or nursing home staff or residents. This type of abuse can include physically tying the senior up or restricting and restraining their movements through drugs or medication. Physical abuse often shows up as visible injuries, according to WebMD. But there may be other signals, including unexplained burns, cuts, bruises, and bleeding; sprained or broken bones; repeated injuries; and a reluctance to see a doctor about their wounds.[32]

Victims often suffer in silence, and when asked about obvious bruising, they may say, "It is nothing." They may not want to reveal the abuse because of embarrassment or to avoid the attention it will bring that could show their incompetence. Because of age and mental capacity, these seniors may not have the ability to comprehend or explain how they were physically injured. Some injuries to seniors are blamed on accidental falls, especially in nursing homes, but may be intentionally caused by the nursing home personnel; these often go unquestioned unless a lawsuit is involved. A June 2022 article by the World Health Organization reports that "a review of recent studies on abuse of older people in institutional settings indicates that 64.2% of staff reported perpetrating some form of abuse in the past year."[33]

Senior citizens often live by themselves and may become highly dependent on their caregivers to attend to simple tasks like eating, bathing, washing, changing clothes, and grocery shopping. Frail seniors are vulnerable and may not be able to defend themselves against younger and stronger caregivers.

---

[32] https://www.webmd.com/healthy-aging/elder-abuse-signs
[33] https://www.who.int/news-room/fact-sheets/detail/abuse-of-older-people

My mom, Carmela, was in a rehabilitation nursing home to get therapy for pneumonia and other issues. My sister and I took turns every day making sure we visited her and stayed with her a minimum of fourteen hours a day, only going home when visiting hours were over. One night, my sister called at 4:00 a.m. and said our mom had been rushed to the hospital emergency room with a severe gash on her forehead. The laceration above her eye was closed with fifteen stitches. The nurse claimed she fell when she got out of bed. My mom had never been able to get up on her own—ever. My mom passed away three days later from her injury; we will never know the truth about what happened. The nursing home never claimed responsibility, let alone apologized for what happened to my mom.

## PSYCHOLOGICAL AND EMOTIONAL ABUSE

Psychological and emotional abuse a senior citizen endures is sometimes hard to detect. A family member, relative, neighbor, or caregiver may be responsible for intentionally causing the senior citizen to experience emotional pain and stress, especially by isolating them from others. Seniors may experience harassment through threatening words and gestures, intimidation, insults, or humiliation. In my opinion, psychological and emotional distress caused by a family member is the catalyst for a senior to possibly give up their will to live. They most often rather die because they cannot take the tormenting abuse any longer.

## FINANCIAL EXPLOITATION

There is an old saying that money is the root of all evil, and it has been known as the great divider of many families. Financial exploitation occurs when any person deliberately tries to take control of a senior citizen's financial accounts through coercion or deception. A vast majority of senior citizens are trusting and may never fathom that someone will try to take advantage of them, especially because of their age. It is inevitable that as we grow older, our mind and brain functions are not as good as they once were, and many senior citizens have difficulty with memory and retaining pertinent information. Many con artists realize that seniors make a great target because they often have money in their accounts and are the least likely to tell anyone if they have been the victim of a crime.

Deceit and manipulation are prevalent in many financial exploitation cases. Caregivers have been known to take advantage of vulnerable older individuals. This often occurs by fraudulently trying to control and manipulate the money the senior has saved throughout their life. A dishonest caregiver may be the person who threatens the senior if they do not cooperate, but strangers are not always the issue seniors have to worry about. Their own greedy adult children or a friend or relative may be the culprit in their financial demise by taking advantage of their money situation. By using legal guardianship or a power of attorney, a family member may try to take control of their grandparents', parents', or relatives' monetary wealth. It is not uncommon to have a dishonest family member, who often lives with the senior, manipulate the older person into putting them in the senior's will or trust, name them as the person to inherit the senior's property, or become the sole beneficiary to the senior's insurance policies.

Another form of financial exploitation is actual theft of a senior citizen's credit cards or money from their checking or savings accounts. The senior may be coerced through the threat of being left alone or abandoned if they are not cooperative. In some cases, a manipulative family member will borrow money from their parent or relative but will not pay it back, with the intention of letting the senior die without any restitution.

## NEGLECT

The tide has turned, especially for women. Though they once took care of the family, now they may need their family to help take care of them. I remember my grandmother saying, "A mother can take care of twelve children, but twelve children often cannot take care of their mom." I find that relatively true; most adult children are busy raising a family, going to work, and living their lives. Children who reside in a different city or state may only see their parent(s) on special occasions and holidays. This is often a recipe for unintentional neglect, but more troubling is intentional neglect.

Seniors often depend on a caregiver, friend, or neighbor to assist them. Many seniors often are placed into senior care facilities, either by their own choice or because they no longer have the ability to care for themselves. The senior is often at the mercy of the facility's staff, and neglect often occurs when the caregiver or senior care facility does not respond to what the senior needs or wants. This is an intentional disregard for the needs of a senior and may include withholding food, drink, medications, or health services for no reason or in retaliation for their behavior. The neglect is real, as many seniors suffer in silence. They may not have the ability to communicate the knowing and intentional acts that can put them at risk and harm them emotionally and physically.

According to the DOJ, a few warning signs of neglect include:
- Dehydration, malnutrition, untreated bed sores, and poor personal hygiene
- Unattended or untreated health problems
- Hazardous or unsafe living conditions/arrangements (such as improper wiring, no heat, or no running water)
- Unsanitary and unclean living conditions (such as dirt, fleas, lice on person, soiled bedding, fecal/urine smell, inadequate clothing)
- An elder's report of being neglected[34]

## ABANDONMENT

Leaving a senior alone at a store, park, public location, or hospital is called *elder abandonment*. If a caregiver, friend, relative, or neighbor leaves the senior alone without arranging for their care, this, too, is considered abandonment. The Stano Law Firm in Ohio writes, "Abandoning an elderly person would qualify as abuse by neglect under state statutes. Usually, elderly abandonment can be defined as the deliberate desertion of a senior in need of care, whether by dropping them off at a care facility or leaving them in a public place. Note that just because someone leaves an elderly relative at a care facility, that doesn't mean they haven't abandoned them, especially if they just drop them off and leave them there."[35]

---

[34] https://www.justice.gov/elderjustice/red-flags-elder-abuse-0
[35] https://stanolaw.com/elderly-abandonment-issue-avoid/

It takes a special person to work with and care for a senior, even if they are healthy. They require a tremendous amount of attention. This can become extremely frustrating and demanding, especially if the elderly patient relies on their caregiver for everything. I have found in many families that siblings often rely on someone in their family to take the lead in caring for an aging parent or relative. I feel the biggest complaint is that all siblings are expected to give their fair share to help, but that often does not happen. Many family arguments occur over the lack of providing the personal or financial assistance their loved one needs. If you have the responsibility of caring for a senior, especially if you feel overwhelmed, consider working with an estate planning attorney to manage all aspects of the senior's care and finances.

## SEXUAL ABUSE

Elder sexual assault occurs more frequently than most people realize. Sexual abuse among senior citizens happens often, especially with an older population that cannot communicate or give their consent willingly.

There are many different forms of sexual abuse committed against senior citizens. It also includes prostitution, showing a senior pornographic material or forcing them to watch sexual acts, and coercing them to undress and expose themselves. Elder sexual abuse includes any type of inappropriate or lewd sexual behavior that is nonconsensual. This includes lascivious and lustful touching or contact with the elder's breasts, buttocks, genitals, or genital area without their approval, consent, or knowledge of such inappropriate behavior.

Numerous sexual abusers prey on elderly victims who show signs of confusion, dementia, mental illness, frailty, or incapacitating medical illness. This makes senior citizens more vulnerable than the average person. Sexual abusers also target seniors who may not be able to communicate well or may not be believed even if they do try to come forward to reveal sexual abuse. A 2015 literature review of sexual abuse of older nursing home residents in *Nursing Research and Practice* estimated that 4 to 6 percent of older adults suffer sexual assault in an institution like a nursing home.[36]

---

[36] https://doi.org/10.1155/2015/902515

Currently, only about 30 percent of victims in this age group report these crimes to the authorities, and nearly 83 percent of all elder sexual abuse victims live in a nursing home or other type of institutional care center.[37] According to the DOJ, the warning signs of elder sexual abuse include bruising around the breasts or genitals, venereal disease, or genital infections, and unexplained vaginal or anal bleeding. There may be changes in an older adult's demeanor, such as showing fear or becoming withdrawn when a specific person is around. Other signs of sexual abuse include evidence of pornographic material being shown to an older adult with diminished capabilities, evidence of blood found on sheets, linens, or an older adult's clothing, and an older adult's report of being sexually assaulted or raped.[38]

In my research, I have discovered that elders who have experienced sexual abuse are more prone to panic attacks and post-traumatic stress. This may include depression and mood swings. It is not uncommon for sexually abused seniors to either become aggressive or to become emotionally withdrawn. In my opinion, they become frustrated that many people, including family, do not believe what they are saying. I find it difficult to comprehend how many people disbelieve what a senior might have experienced as fictional.

## SELF-NEGLECT

It is easy to understand how a senior loses their ability to take care of the basic needs to survive. "Although elder self-neglect doesn't involve a third-party perpetrator, it's still considered a form of elder abuse that raises serious health and safety concerns. In fact, most reported cases of elder abuse involve elder self-neglect."[39] They struggle to be independent and may have difficulty getting to the grocery store and eating healthy, cleaning their house, and remembering to take medications. Self-neglect is often one of the most overlooked forms of elder abuse and is often exacerbated by the senior's lack of trust in anyone who tries to help them.

---

[37] https://www.nursinghomeabusecenter.com/elder-abuse/types/sexual-abuse/
[38] https://www.justice.gov/elderjustice/red-flags-elder-abuse-0
[39] https://www.findlaw.com/elder/elder-abuse/elder-self-neglect.html

Some seniors have no one to turn to. They may not have any family or friends who care about them or live close to them. Police officers throughout our nation are called out daily to check on the well-being of someone who has not been seen or heard from for quite some time. When an officer does respond and investigates this type of call, they may find a senior who is in need of medical attention or who is living in squalor. FindLaw.com recommends,

> "If you suspect a case of elder self-neglect, contact your local Adult Protective Services office for further guidance. APS offices provide social services to abused, neglected, or exploited elders or adults with certain disabilities. To find the APS office near you, see the National Adult Protective Services Association, which provides a list of APS offices nationwide."[40]

---

[40] https://www.findlaw.com/elder/elder-abuse/elder-self-neglect.html

# CHAPTER 10

# OFFICE SAFETY AND WORKPLACE VIOLENCE

*"Safety has to be everyone's responsibility . . . Everyone needs to know that they are empowered to speak up if there is an issue."*
Captain Scott Kelly

EVERYONE EXPECTS THE company they work for to do its due diligence to keep employees safe, but there are a number of reasons for violence at the workplace. A disgruntled employee may want to get even with their coworkers, management, or their immediate boss. There could be issues between employees and customers that go awry. There are dozens of reasons that could cause a person to want to harass, torment, or inflict pain on someone at work.

A person's clothing may mask their true intentions. Someone wearing a suit and tie in an office environment may be thought of as "another person in the corporate office" and may not appear as a threat. If that same person were dressed in dirty and raggedy clothes, he would not only be suspicious to most people but most likely be questioned about what he is doing on-site. Many office personnel would most likely summon security or law enforcement on this type of individual. Yet a thief who is nicely dressed who acts with confidence will appear to be honest and trustworthy. Often, though they are the biggest threat for stealing personal items as they wander throughout a workspace. When approached, they will most likely act lost or say they are on the wrong floor.

An office receptionist should have a code word to alert other employees that they may be in danger, and employees need to call 911 immediately if they hear that code word. I like the acronym NORA, which stands for **N**eed an **O**fficer **R**ight **A**way, because the name "Nora" is not as common as Kathy, Linda, or Sue.

## FIRING AN EMPLOYEE

Debbie Pickus, a mental and physical wellness coach for companies and an expert in office safety, says,

> Having to fire someone is never an easy task for any business owner, HR manager, or supervisor. There should be procedures in place to adapt to any situation, especially if the fired individual becomes angry and violent. My first recommendation is to be prepared for any response from a pleasant ending to the worst-case scenario. You never know how someone will react when faced with the reality that their livelihood will be disrupted. Having empathy for them is necessary for a smooth termination; however, being ready for the worst case is required. Even the most docile and friendly person may snap and become violent or angry. We never know what's going on in someone's life, and this could be the last straw.
>
> It is also important to be aware of extenuating circumstances; has the person being terminated made any previous threats or shown signs of unstable or erratic behavior? Have they ever mentioned owning weapons or spoken about guns?
>
> Schedule the termination meeting in a quiet room away from other employees or personnel. This allows the terminated employee to maintain a level of dignity, not having to do a "walk of shame" in front of coworkers. At the meeting, in addition to the firing manager, there should always be another person, preferably someone with a strong physical presence. They can act as a witness

and relay what took place if requested. It is very important that the firing manager is not alone with the employee.

Not only is it important to terminate an employee in a private location, but the room's décor and seating arrangement should be considered.

Ensure that no small objects such as scissors, metal water bottles, or staplers are close by. They can be used as weapons if the person fired wants to retaliate. Also, be aware of the seating in the room. Guide the terminated employee to a seat that is away from the door. In one case that I remember, the employee being terminated got up and locked the door, then went over to a kitchen area where there was a knife and began threatening the manager. Personal safety rule number one is to make sure you have a clear exit if needed. Common sense is essential during any person's termination. It is important to never schedule a termination in a food prep area where utensils can be used as weapons.

Pickus also stresses the importance of addressing what happens after the employee receives notice of their termination.

A policy should be in place for how a terminated employee will gather their personal belongings. Either someone will pack for them (this will need to be stated in an employee handbook somewhere at hiring), or someone will accompany them to pack their things. This policy will depend on the company itself and the layout of the offices, but it's necessary to make sure that other employees remain safe. This policy will also cover the terminated employee giving up any credentials, keys, or ID cards so they can no longer get into the building. This should be done respectfully. It is imperative that a terminated employee not be able to walk around the facility after they are terminated.

Pickus cited a situation where an HR manager designated another HR manager to terminate a difficult employee, which created a prime example of what not to do.

The terminating manager did not follow procedures and allowed the just-released employee to go around saying goodbye to everyone but lost track of the person for ninety minutes in the building. The HR manager, fearing for her safety, hid in a bathroom stall until security found the terminated employee. Always alert security of any essential details regarding an employee's termination, so they are prepared should something go wrong.

## BOMB THREATS

Bomb threats are often made to scare and disrupt or cause fear to an individual, company, organization, or religious institution. This may be from a disgruntled employee or someone who may hold a grudge. In my experience, if a person really wants to hurt someone, they most likely will do so without any warning. Most common bomb threats are via phone calls, emails, or handwritten notes.

My suggestion is to stay calm if you're the recipient of a verbal or written bomb threat. Listen carefully, and write down as much information as you can. If the phone has a display, take the number down immediately. Notify authorities (911) from a different phone if possible. Many authorities recommend not using cell phones in the immediate area. Alert supervisors and management, even if you're instructed not to. Every bomb threat is unique. The credibility of the threat needs to be assessed diligently.

I handled only one bomb threat in my police career, which was located at a doctor's office. It was scary and nerve-wracking, especially when the doctor ran a block away before we got there. A small, frail receptionist finally decided to go into the office with us. We shut off our police radios and carefully searched every room in the office. We asked her if there were any suspicious packages or if anything unusual was left behind that day. Even though most bomb threats are hoaxes meant to scare or disrupt a business or event, my partner and I only thought about "what if." Luckily, nothing happened. The doctor left his employees and went home for the day. My partner said, "Great boss, glad I don't work for him." My thought on bomb threats: if a person really wanted to hurt someone, they would not warn them of impending danger but just use the element of surprise.

## MAIL ROOMS

Many offices located on large commercial properties have mail rooms that handle packages on a daily basis. The workers are often trained to look out for any suspicious packages. Here are a few tips if a package is delivered to your office other than the office building. Be suspicious of any package that has been sitting for a while. Question a package with no return address, one with stains or a strange odor or noise or one that ticks. Be suspicious of excessive or foreign postage, poor handwriting, misspelled words or names on the label, or anything marked personal or confidential.

## OTHER TYPES OF WORKPLACE VIOLENCE

Workplace violence can include any type of abusive or offensive language or false, malicious, or unfounded statements. Report this behavior immediately to management.

The DOJ recognizes workplace violence as a specific category of violent crime. Workplace violence can be defined as an intentional work-related act that inflicts or attempts to inflict bodily harm on another person, whether committed by an employee, contractor, vendor, visitor, or client. This includes physical assaults such as striking or pushing, aggressive physical acts, and being sworn or shouted at.

The National Institute for Occupational Safety and Health (NIOSH) lists four different types of workplace violence categories:

1. Criminal intent: a violent act by criminals who have no connection to the workplace. The perpetrator enters to commit robbery or another crime. An example of this would be a robbery at a convenience store or bank.
2. Violence directed at an employee by customers, clients, patients, students, inmates, or any others who provide services; an example would be a customer at a grocery store fighting with the manager.

3. Violence against coworkers, supervisors, or managers by a present or former employee; an example of this is a person who was fired and comes back to the workplace with a weapon to kill or hurt the person who fired them.
4. Violence committed in the workplace by someone who doesn't work there but has a personal relationship with an employee; an example is an abusive spouse or domestic partner who comes to the workplace to cause harm to their partner or anyone else who gets involved.[41]

Communication is key to developing a climate and attitude of trust and respect in the workplace. Management should always have a goal threat assessment in place. Employers should recognize and have a proactive plan in place for any signs of discourteous conduct, such as throwing or pushing objects, punching walls, and slamming doors, and employees should be trained in precautions to take for each scenario.

## ADDITIONAL OFFICE SAFETY TIPS

- Notify security personnel of any suspicious people or vehicles in the area, especially after normal working hours.
- Keep emergency phone numbers to call police, fire, and security at every phone location.
- Plan and memorize escape routes.
- Keep potential weapons like scissors, letter openers, and paperweights out of the reach of clients.
- Have a list at the front desk available at all times of all employees who are trained in CPR.

---

[41] https://wwwn.cdc.gov/WPVHC/Nurses/Course/Slide/Unit1_5

## — CHAPTER 11 —

# ACTIVE SHOOTER

*"Only with gun violence do we respond to repeated tragedies by saying that mourning is acceptable but preventing more tragedies is not. But that's unacceptable. As others have observed, talking about how to stop a mass shooting in the aftermath of a string of mass shootings isn't 'too soon.' It's much too late."*
Ezra Klein

AN ACTIVE SHOOTER is a person who aggressively tries to kill individuals in a confined space in a populated area or office, most often using an automatic weapon or shotgun. It is sad to say that active shooter incidents have become more frequent than in previous years. The incident evolves quickly and is often over within minutes. Active shooters usually continue to move throughout a building or area until stopped by law enforcement or by suicide.

In many instances, an active shooter is motivated by revenge, rage, anger, or hate. An active shooter may have a grudge against an individual person or company. In their mind, they may feel they have been humiliated, picked on, bullied, or unfairly laid off or fired from their job. Their intent is to get even for the pain they have endured. The active shooter may target one individual but will often shoot at anyone they encounter in their random act of trying to accomplish their goal. They may have a strong belief or ideology in their mind that justifies their actions.

Not every active shooter has a specific person in mind to hurt or kill; they may feel the need to change society. They may believe that everyone is evil, or they may have a strong belief or ideology that they believe justifies their actions. An active shooter with this intention may be a religious zealot who believes they were told to kill by God, the devil, or Allah. They may fantasize about killing for no specific reason.

Active shooters often kill themselves or are killed by law enforcement after their killing spree is over. I often speculate about what caused these troubled individuals to follow the demons that ravaged their minds. Did they believe their actions would end in infamy because of the news coverage throughout the world? Was it a copycat behavior for notoriety, a quick claim to fame? Was it because the active shooter had low self-esteem or felt worthless? It is difficult to surmise what actually is going through an active shooter's mind before and in the aftermath of their destruction. They may feel that they cannot live with whatever emotional pain they are experiencing and have no way out but to kill. In the end, they may feel that they are the real victim.

## SCHOOL SHOOTINGS

At one time unheard of, school shootings are today a too-frequent occurrence. One of the first widely covered school shooting incidents occurred at Columbine High School in Littleton, Colorado, on April 20, 1999. Students Eric Harris and Dylan Klebold murdered twelve students and one teacher, and twenty-one additional individuals were injured. It was one of the deadliest school shootings in US history.

Security.org reports that "Since the Columbine massacre, there have been a total of 304 fatal school shootings and counting,"[42] and the Associated Press reports, "Fourteen mass shootings at US schools since 1999's massacre at Columbine High School in Colorado have killed a total of 169 victims,"[43] including the massacre at Robb Elementary School in Uvalde, Texas, which is still under investigation at the time of this writing. Community members are understandably reeling after a mass-shooting event, especially when victims are young children.

---

[42] https://www.security.org/blog/a-timeline-of-school-shootings-since-columbine/
[43] https://www.usnews.com/news/us/articles/2022-05-24/a-look-at-some-of-the-deadliest-us-school-shootings

# PROTECTING YOURSELF DURING AN ACTIVE SHOOTER EVENT

The Department of Homeland Security (DHS) and the FBI consider active shooters the greatest terrorist threat on campuses, in buildings, and in our communities. DHS suggests three important tactics to keep yourself safe: *Run*, *Hide*, and *Fight*.[44] As they explain, your actions can be the difference between surviving and dying. First and foremost, remain calm so you make thoughtful and efficient decisions.

## *Run*

When an active shooter is in the area, get out of the line of fire. Everyone's first priority should be to get out of the building or office safely and follow your company's emergency exit plan. If there is an escape path, attempt to evacuate. In this type of situation, not everyone may want to leave the area. If you feel that it is better to evacuate, do so whether others agree to it or not. Leave your valuables behind except for your cell phone—try to take your cell phone if you can. Try to help others escape if possible, and once outside, do your best to prevent others from going into the area. Last, call 911 when you are safe.

## *Hide*

If the situation warrants and evacuation is not possible, try to find a secure room and lock the door. If you are in a room that does not have a door that locks, block the door with the largest, heaviest item possible and position yourself out of sight. Use something to protect you that might offer additional protection, such as a wall, desk, or file cabinet. Silence your phone, stay calm, and remain as quiet as possible. Keep as close to the floor as possible and keep out of the shooter's view. Be careful not to limit your escape options, and stay away from windows.

## *Fight*

Fight an assailant only as a last resort and only if your life is in danger. If you choose to fight, it is important to commit to your actions completely and

---

[44] https://www.fbi.gov/resources/active-shooter-safety-resources

act with strength and aggression. Try to disarm, disable, or incapacitate the shooter. Improvise and use any object available as a weapon. Even a pen can be used as a stabbing instrument.

## *Until Law Enforcement Arrives*

The job of the first responders is to stop the shooter. Because of this, rescue efforts will be delayed until the shooter is stopped. Any injured victims will be taken care of, and it is important you do not attempt to move them. Officers are unsure about who is the shooter and who isn't, and it is important to stay safe in this situation as well. Keep your hands visible at all times, and avoid pointing or yelling.

When an emergency occurs, customers and visitors will look to employees to direct them to safety since those are the people familiar with the building and workspace. Office buildings should always have an emergency action plan in place and a shelter-in-place area designated within the facility. Employees and customers are likely to follow the lead of managers or uniformed officials during an emergency situation. Managers should remain calm and professional and take immediate action and be prepared to lead. One of the first things a manager can do is evacuate employees and customers through a viable, preplanned evacuation route to a safe area and make sure to lock and barricade doors.

The US Department of Labor's Occupational Safety and Health Administration (OSHA) has an emergency action plan on its website. At a minimum, the plan must include but is not limited to the following elements:

- Means of reporting fires and other emergencies
- Evacuation procedures and emergency escape route assignments
- Procedures for employees who remain to operate critical plant operations before they evacuate
- Accounting for all employees after an emergency evacuation has been completed
- Rescue and medical duties for employees performing them
- Names or job titles of persons who can be contacted

Although they are not specifically required by OSHA, you may find it helpful to include the following in your plan:

- A description of the alarm system to be used to notify employees (including disabled employees) to evacuate or take other actions. The alarms used for different actions should be distinctive and might include horn blasts, sirens, or even public address systems.
- The site of an alternative communications center to be used in the event of a fire or explosion.
- A secure on- or offsite location to store originals or duplicate copies of accounting records, legal documents, your employees' emergency contact lists, and other essential records.[45]

---

[45] https://www.osha.gov/etools/evacuation-plans-procedures/eap/minimum-requirements

# Conclusion

CRIME AND INJUSTICE have been issues throughout history. Millions of victims have suffered emotionally, physically, and monetarily. Criminals thrive on opportunity. Laws have been enacted, and police forces have been formed to suppress and control criminal activity, especially situations that endanger innocent people and that lead to violence and death. Without laws and rules, we would experience near-continual chaos, pandemonium, and confusion.

Most Americans are law-abiding people who care about their fellow citizens. In my opinion, a majority of the time, it is a small percentage of individuals who are enmeshed in criminal activity and behavior.

Greed and self-indulgence are often the principal components that lead to immoral and criminal behavior. If a criminal or thief spots an opportunity to take advantage of someone, they will. I hope that in writing this book, I have given everyone the tools to defeat a criminal from causing harm to you, your family, or your property. I sincerely hope this book will assist you in becoming more aware of your surroundings and diligent in not making yourself a victim of any crime.

Many scams are deceiving millions of people on a daily basis. Just walk away.

Thank you for giving me the opportunity to spread the word about staying prepared at home, at work, and on the street and for reading my book. Please stay safe; your life may depend on it!

Dr. Ron Rufo

## Acknowledgments

A sincere thank you to the many contributors and experts who have been gracious enough to provide provocative insights, thoughts, and solutions for this book on street safety. I am truly grateful for your thoughtfulness and contributions.

To Candace Johnson, a well-known and respected editor. I am very fortunate to have been introduced to Candace. Her guidance, dedication, and support have gone above and beyond all my expectations. Candace, I appreciate your time and expertise; you are amazing. I am proud and humbled to call you my friend.

To Michelle Booth, a brilliant and talented proofreader who did an excellent job on my book. She was patient, thorough, and detailed. Michelle, I appreciate your time and expertise.

To Kim Martin from Jera Publishing for her guidance and direction. Kim is very knowledgeable and makes sure everything is done in a professional manner.

To Ronald Cruz, a very talented artist who did an excellent job creating my book cover. Thank you for an outstanding job.

To Paul Scarlato for your advice, thoughts, and suggestions, which are excellent. Paul, you are very talented and knowledgeable. I am glad we are friends.

To Lynne Ansani for being a dear friend and sharing her story.

To Matt May for writing the Foreword and for being a great friend.

# Resources

**Center for the Study and Prevention of Violence**
cspv@colorado.edu

Institute of Behavioral Science
University of Colorado Boulder
483 UCB
Boulder, CO 80309-0483
303-735-3655

**CharityNavigator**
https://www.charitynavigator.org

Charity Navigator is one of the largest independent nonprofit and charitable assessors on the internet. CharityNavigator actively encourages nonprofits to update information on its site.
299 Market Street, Suite 250
Saddle Brook, NJ 07663

**CharityWatch**
https://www.charitywatch.org

CharityWatch is an independent charity watchdog group. They claim to let a person know how efficiently a charity will use a person's donation they want to support. CharityWatch does not allow any input from the nonprofits it rates.

**Credit Bureaus**

**Equifax**  Equifax.com
1-866-640-2273  General Customer Service
1-888-766-0008  To place a fraud alert
1-800-685-1111  To order a special report

**Experian**  Experian.com
1-888-EXPERIAN
(1-888 397-3742)  To place a fraud alert
1-800-831-5614  Customer support
1-800-854-7201  Technical support

**TransUnion**  Transunion.com
1-800-680-7289  Trans Union Fraud Victim Assistance
1-800-916-8800 or
1-800-813-5604  Customer service
1-800-909-8872  To freeze or unfreeze credit

**Federal Bureau of Investigation (FBI)**
**Internet Crime Complaint Center (IC3)**
https://www.ic3.gov
https://www.fbi.gov/investigate/cyber
https://tips.fbi.gov

The Internet Crime Complaint Center is the nation's central hub for reporting cybercrime. It is run by the FBI, the lead federal agency for investigating cybercrime. 935 Pennsylvania Ave, NW, Washington, DC 20535
1-800-225-5324/1-800-Call-FBI

**Federal Trade Commission (FTC)**
https://www.identitytheft.gov/#/ or
https://consumer.ftc.gov/features/identity-theft to report identity theft
https://www.donotcall.gov to report unwanted calls
https://reportfraud.ftc.gov/#/ to report fraud, scams and bad business practices.

The Federal Trade Commission (FTC) is a bipartisan federal agency that enforces antitrust laws and protects consumers. Their activities include investigating fraud or false advertising, congressional inquiries, and pre-merger notification.
600 Pennsylvania Avenue, NW, Washington DC, 20580
(202) 236-2222

**Federal Emergency Management Administration (FEMA)**
https://www.fema.gov

FEMA's mission is helping people before, during, and after disasters.
P.O. Box 10055
Hyattsville, MD 20782-8055
1-800-621-3362

**Financial Industry Regulatory Authority (FINRA)**
https:/www.fnra.org

FINRA is a government-authorized not-for-profit organization that oversees U.S. broker-dealers to protect investors and ensure the market's integrity.
301-590-6500

**National Adult Protective Services Association**
https://www.napsa-now.org

The National Adult Protective Services Association (NAPSA) is a national nonprofit 501 (c)(3)organization with members in all fifty states. Formed in 1989, the goal of NAPSA is to provide Adult Protective Services (APS) programs a forum for sharing information, solving problems, and improving the quality of services for victims of elder and vulnerable adult mistreatment.
1612 K Street NW #200, Washington, DC 20006
(202) 370-6292

**National Center on Elder Abuse (NCEA)**
https://ncea.acl.gov/

The NCEA provides the latest information regarding research, training, best practices, news, and resources on elder abuse, neglect, and exploitation to professionals and the public.

c/o University of Southern California Keck School of Medicine
Department of Family Medicine and Geriatrics
1000 South Fremont Avenue, Unit 22, Building A-6
Alhambra, CA 91803
1-855-500-3537 (ELDR)

**US Department of Justice, Office of Justice Programs (OJP)**
https://www.ojp.gov/programs/identitytheft

810 7th Street NW, Washington, DC, 20531
202-514-2000

**Office for Victims of Crime**
https://ovc.ojp.gov

Expanding services to reach victims of ID theft and financial fraud.

## Contributors and Experts

**David Anderson:** David is the Police Chief of the DesPlaines (Illinois) Police Department. He has over thirty years of police service and is a highly respected law enforcement leader. David has a bachelor's in criminal justice management from Aurora University, a master's in organizational behavior from Benedictine University, and is currently working toward a PhD in organization development at Benedictine University.

**Daniel Banicki:** Dan is currently a sergeant with the St. Joseph County Police Department in South Bend, Indiana. He has been in law enforcement for more than twenty-six years.

**Lenny Cacioppo:** Len is a retired Chicago Police officer with over thirty years of service; he was an HBT SWAT Sniper, a Special Operations officer, and a firearms technician.

**Billy Cinkay:** Bill is a former police sergeant who worked in the western suburbs of Chicago. He now works as an Outreach Specialist dedicating his life to saving first responders who suffer from substance abuse and mental health issues.

**John Doherty:** John has been a member of the Chicago Police Department for thirty-six years and is currently serving as a captain in the 22nd District. John has earned two masters degrees, one in security analysis and the other in leadership and supervision. He has received more than 105 department awards along with numerous certificates of recognition. John was assigned to many specialized units and earned numerous certificates when given the opportunity to attend several advanced leadership and investigative training courses.

**Michael Duck:** Mike is a retired Chicago Police Officer with over eighteen years of service and spent most of his career as a Preventive Programs speaker on safety. He is a youth program board member, coach, and mentor. Mike earned his MBA from Saint Xavier University.

**Fernando (Frank) Flores:** Frank is a retired commander of the Illinois State Police and has served in law enforcement for over thirty-five years. During his career, he specialized in critical infrastructure protection, specifically for government facilities and employees. Frank developed and conducted numerous programs in active shooter, crisis intervention, personal safety, and workplace security.

**Michael Franzese:** Michael is an author, speaker, and former captain in the Colombo crime family. He has a YouTube channel of videos about his life in the Costa Nostra and how his life changed when he found Christ.

**Adrienne Gardner:** Adrienne is currently a lieutenant of police for the Richmond, Virginia Police Department. She has a master's degree in criminal justice from Virginia Commonwealth University.

**Ken Grandy:** Ken had the pleasure of a thirty-year career as a proud member in various tactical, gang, weapon, and narcotic units of the Chicago Police Department. His career culminated as a detective in the Robbery, Burglary, and Theft division. Ken was the director of security at Hyatt and W hotel properties, and he developed security staffing and training for a nationwide security firm where he is still a consultant.

**Andrew Hock:** Andy is the deputy chief of police of the Elmwood Park Police Department. He is a graduate of Northwestern University School of Police

Staff and Command. Andy currently serves on several boards and committees that form a partnership between the community and law enforcement.

**Mark Lasky:** Mark is a chief security officer for Secure Tech Solutions (STS) in Chicago. He is a veteran in the security industry with more than forty years of experience developing integrated security plans and solutions for many major business and corporate clients throughout the Chicagoland area. Mark also is a regular consultant for law enforcement and legal communities, providing expert testimony in forensic evidence.

**Rev. Dr. Kimberly Lewis-Davis:** Kim is a Chicago Police Department chaplain and police officer. She earned her doctorate of ministry degree from United Theological Seminary.

**William R. Looney:** Bill is a retired Chicago Police commander and veteran of the Chicago Police Department, where he served for over thirty-two years. Bill finished his distinguished career as commander of the 16th Police District on the North Side of Chicago.

**Patrick Murphy:** Patrick is in his thirty-second year of service as a police officer and holds a bachelor's degree from Southern Illinois University. Patrick is the chief of police for the Springfield Park District Police Department. He has served as a certified defensive tactics instructor in all fifty States and Canada.

**David Nance:** David has been the CEO and president of SABRE, the number one preferred brand of pepper spray and personal safety solutions used by consumers and law enforcement worldwide since 2001. David is a nationally acclaimed safety expert dedicated to educating law enforcement officers and the public about personal safety. He started the SABRE Law Enforcement Training Division and the SABRE Personal Safety Academy featuring the Civilian Safety Awareness Program and the College Safety Program. David has also been a guest speaker at various industry trade shows and is a member of the National Crime Prevention Council.

**Rose Oliveri:** Rose is a twenty-six-year veteran of the Chicago Police Department and was one of the first women to be assigned to the Patrol Division. Rose is a consummate professional in street safety, working twenty-two of her twenty-six-year career as a crime prevention officer. She conducted thousands of street safety programs for the citizens of Chicago and appeared on numerous local and national shows, including *Oprah* and *Nightline*.

**Henry Perez:** Henry is a retired Chicago Police officer who served most of his career as a dedicated senior citizen service officer and community relations mentor in the 10th District.

**Debbie Pickus:** Debbie teaches individuals and groups how to harness their mental and physical power to create confidence, energy, and success in business and personal life. She is the founder and CEO of Team Fireball, a coaching and training company.

**Eugene J. Roy:** Gene is a retired chief of detectives for the Chicago Police Department. He is a consultant on public safety and investigations throughout the country.

**Frank Scarpa:** Frank is currently a lieutenant for the Richmond, Virginia Police Department with over eighteen years in law enforcement.

**Nick Sposato:** Nick is currently the alderman for the 38th Ward in the city of Chicago. Nick previously served as a firefighter with the Chicago Fire Department for eighteen years.

**William Townsell:** William is a graduate of the University of Illinois and is the assistant director of the Chicago Police Department's Office of Community Policing. In his twenty-year career, he has developed and implemented a myriad of crime and community abatement strategies for residents and stakeholders. William is currently acting supervisor for the civilian field staff of the Community Policing section.

**Bart Tweedie:** Bart is a sergeant with the Mount Prospect Police Department in Illinois. Throughout his nineteen-year career, he has worked as a patrol officer and patrol supervisor, detective, accident investigator, and trainer. Bart is currently the training coordinator for his agency. He has taught control tactics, firearms, field training, and patrol tactics.

**Richard Wistocki:** Rich has been a law enforcement officer for thirty years, twenty-eight of those with the Naperville Police Department. He served as a detective in his last twenty-two years as an internet crimes investigator. He has also been a SWAT operator and sniper. Rich is an instructor for the Department of Justice and various Law Enforcement Mobile Training Units and POST units across the United States. He is also the creator of the Illinois Sexting Law.

**Wilem Wong:** Wilem is a retired New York City Police Department (NYPD) sergeant (Special Assignment) with over twenty-one years of combined creditable service to New York City and New York State. He has worked in NYPD assignments in project and program management, leadership and training development, development of health and wellness initiatives, investigations, and patrol operations. Wilem is a veteran of Operation Iraqi Freedom, having served with US Army Civil Affairs in Iraq and Afghanistan. He earned a master's in management and leadership from Webster University and a bachelor's in finance from New York University.

Printed in the USA
CPSIA information can be obtained
at www.ICGtesting.com
JSHW072116241024
72295JS00006B/12